'This outstanding book presen[...]ch-ology of the internet, analys[...]ity, exposure, control, accessibility [...]ed in an on-line environment. It [...]rce us to re-think our convention[...], relationships, aggression, parenting and group behaviour. The book will be of interest to researchers, students and practitioners not only in psychology, but in all related disciplines as well where the internet changed the way we relate to each other.'

– Joseph Paul Forgas, AM, DPhil, DSc. (Oxford), FASSA,
Scientia Professor of Psychology, University of New South Wales,
Sydney, Australia

'In this important new book Yair Amichai-Hamburger demonstrates his encyclopedic knowledge of this fascinating field of modern psychology. With the same deft touch he takes the reader through a bewildering range of topics – illustrating the good (therapy, romance, and volunteering), the bad (violence) and the ugly (hate forums) – that illustrates the all-encompassing effect of the internet on our daily lives.'

– Miles Hewstone,
Professor of Social Psychology & Public Policy,
University of Oxford

INTERNET PSYCHOLOGY

THE BASICS

We can't imagine our lives without the Internet. It is the tool of our existence; without it we couldn't work, plan our social and leisure activities, and interact with friends. The Internet's influence on contemporary society extends across every aspect of our personal and professional lives, but how has this altered us in psychological terms? How are we to understand how the Internet can promote enormous amounts of caring and kindness to strangers and yet be the source of unremitting acts of terror?

This book, grounded in the latest cutting-edge research, enhances our understanding of how we, and our children, behave online. It explores questions such as:

- Why does our self-control abandon us sometimes on the Internet?
- Why does the Internet create a separate realm of social and personal relationships?
- How does all that change us as people?
- Are young people really as exposed and threatened on the web as people think?

Internet Psychology: The Basics is a vital and fascinating guide to the online world, drawing on classic theories of human behavior to shed fresh light on this central facet of modern life. It argues that, even in an age of constant technological advancement, our understanding of the human psyche remains rooted in these well-established theories. Embracing both positive and negative aspects of Internet use, this easy introduction to the subject will appeal to students and general readers alike.

Yair Amichai-Hamburger received his PhD from Oxford University. He is a Professor of Psychology and Communication, and the Director of the Research Centre for Internet Psychology (CIP) in Herzliya, Israel. He has written widely on the impact of the Internet on wellbeing, and is credited as being one of the earliest commentators to note the potential power and significance of online social networks. He has received awards from the American Library and the Academy of Management.

THE BASICS SERIES TITLES

Coming Soon

BIOETHICS: THE BASICS
2ND EDITION
BY ALASTAIR V. CAMPBELL

SEMIOTICS: THE BASICS
3RD EDITION
BY DANIEL CHANDLER

CONTEMPORARY INDIA: THE BASICS
BY REKHA DATTA

RHETORIC: THE BASICS
MICHAEL BURKE

Available Now

FORENSIC PSYCHOLOGY: THE BASICS
BY SANDIE TAYLOR

SPORT PSYCHOLOGY: THE BASICS
BY DAVID TOD

MEDIA STUDIES: THE BASICS
BY JULIAN MCDOUGALL

SOCIOLOGY: THE BASICS
2ND EDITION
BY KEN PLUMMER

CRIMINOLOGY: THE BASICS
3RD EDITION
BY SANDRA WALKLATE

ARTIFICIAL INTELLIGENCE: THE BASICS
BY KEVIN WARWICK

GENDER: THE BASICS
BY HILARY LIPS

DISCOURSE: THE BASICS
BY ANGELA GODDARD, NEIL CAREY

SOCIAL WORK: THE BASICS
BY MARK DOEL

HUMAN GENETICS: THE BASICS
2ND EDITION
BY RICKI LEWIS

CRITICAL THINKING: THE BASICS
BY STUART HANSCOMB

MODERNISM: THE BASICS
BY LAURA WINKIEL

OLOGY

THE BASICS

Yair Amichai-Hamburger

Routledge
Taylor & Francis Group

LONDON AND NEW YORK

First published 2017
by Routledge
2 Park Square, Milton Park, Abingdon, Oxon OX14 4RN

and by Routledge
711 Third Avenue, New York, NY 10017

Routledge is an imprint of the Taylor & Francis Group, an informa business

© 2017 Yair Amichai-Hamburger

British Library Cataloguing in Publication Data
A catalogue record for this book is available from the British Library

Library of Congress Cataloguing in Publication Data
A catalog record for this book has been requested.

ISBN: 978-1-138-65605-5 (hbk)
ISBN: 978-1-138-65606-2 (pbk)
ISBN: 978-1-315-62216-3 (ebk)

Typeset in Bembo Std
by Out of House Publishing

Dedicated to my mother-in-law, Carole, the matriarch
of our family, and to our first granddaughter,
Adi Naomi, the first of her generation in our family

CONTENTS

ACKNOWLEDGMENTS

To start, I would like to thank my wife, Debbie. Everything starts and ends with her; I would not be able to make it without her. I would like to say a large thank you to our wonderful children and children-in-law, who really know how much time and effort has gone into this project. I am very grateful to John Cohen, a family friend who has been close to us over many years. John was exceptionally supportive of the idea for this book and assisted in many ways to make it happen. I am also very grateful for the large role played by Susan Goodman, another valued friend. Her advice and hard work on earlier versions of the manuscript were extremely important in making the book materialize. Another very large thank you goes to Rebecca Sacks. A chance meeting at a Friday night dinner in New York led to a fruitful collaboration and what I hope will be an enduring friendship. Rebecca worked on a later version of the book and I value her ideas and professionalism that helped give it its final shape. My thanks go, too, to my research colleagues, Shir Etgar, Shaul Fox, Zack Hyatt, Tal Shani Sherman, and Barry Schneider. My deep appreciation goes to Tal Ben-Shahar, a good friend and colleague, who encouraged me to write my last book, *The Good, the Bad and the Ugly: The Psychology of Life on the Internet*, which was published in Hebrew in 2013. This work formed the basis for the current book, as I realized from the feedback I received on the former, how important and valuable a comprehensive integration of psychology is for Internet users.

It is important for me to acknowledge the Wikipedia project, which is one of the best illustrations of how the wisdom of many individuals can become a phenomenal, integrated data bank. This project has taught me how to utilize the human resource of the Internet to produce prosocial change.

PREFACE

It is hard to believe that, like many other fine inventions, the Internet was conceived by accident. It came to life in the 1960s, at a time when the superpowers were at the height of their arms race. Filled with the spirit of the times, researchers at the US Department of Defense were preparing for the worst. They wanted to develop a form of communications that could keep its data unharmed through a nuclear holocaust. They believed that if all the important data was centralized in one location, it would be vulnerable to a single attack. So, with a view to preserving the data, they scattered it throughout a large computer network. The idea being that if data were destroyed in one location, they could be reconstructed from elsewhere. Time passed, and that decentralized military computer network evolved into an academic network. From there to today's Internet, the journey was a short one.

I started working in the field of Internet psychology in 1998. At that point, I had noticed that psychologists had almost nothing to say about the Internet, despite the fact that psychology was integrally linked to it. In 1999, at a festive cocktail gathering at the psychology department where I then worked, I was approached by one of the department's most prominent professors. He leaned magisterially in my direction, and using a stage whisper, so he could be clearly heard by everyone around, he said, "Yair, can you tell me what on earth psychology has to do with the Internet?" His tone was scathing; this was clearly a rhetorical question. At that point I understood that by taking an interest in the connection between psychology and the Internet, I had violated an unspoken boundary. The professor saw himself as representing the science of psychology: a field that seeks to understand the human mind and behavior in a manner quite separate from the exact sciences; conversely, computers are all about technology and machinery.

Early on, my preliminary research in Internet psychology led me to change my whole professional focus. Since then, I've invested all my energy into understanding how the Internet influences our lives. The topic interested and excited me from the first day I approached it, and it still does. I believe strongly that where there are people, there is psychology, and the Internet is generated by the people who use it. Since that whisper from the professor, nineteen years have passed and thousands of articles have appeared all looking at various components of a question that is anything but rhetorical: "What has psychology got to do with the Internet?"

What indeed. The Internet is an inherent part of our lives. We do almost everything via the Internet – checking the weather in the morning in order to dress appropriately, making hotel reservations for a London holiday, or organizing our social arrangements; as professionals, we use it to keep up with our own specialized fields. For children and young people, born into a digital world, Internet use is as much a part of life as drinking water and breathing air.

When we try to understand the influence technology has on our lives, we face certain challenges. First, it must be noted that technology in general, and the Internet in particular, are dynamic forces that are continually changing. Between the time of writing this book and your reading it, new sites and apps will have sprung up with technologies that didn't exist before. Second, we are also so deeply involved in our digital lives that trying to pause and understand the effect technology is having on us is almost like the challenge of standing motionless and trying to comprehend the effects of our breathing or our heart rate. Despite these difficulties, it is vital that we comprehend the impact that such omnipresent technology has on our lives, particularly on the quality of our well-being and our relationships.

It is only by pausing to understand this digital transformation that we can begin to take control, tame the beast, and create appropriate boundaries. Vital to understanding human behavior on the Internet is the ability to make psychological observations. By focusing on the human mind, we glean insights that can serve us long after the rise and fall of various online fads.

Today, as head of the Research Center for Internet Psychology (CIP) at the Interdisciplinary Center (IDC) Herzliya, I am proud to have participated in staking out this important new scientific field. I feel that the time has come to write a book that responds comprehensively with an explanation of how psychology relates to the Internet.

The book opens, in Chapter 1, by seeking answers to the issue of what makes the Internet a unique psychological environment. It continues on to Chapter 2, considering how the personality of individual users is relevant to what they do on the net and whether therapy online can truly be effective. Next, in Chapter 3 we take a look at romance in the digital age; how it has changed and to what extent it has remained as it always was. Chapter 4 investigates why the violent aspects of human behavior play out so readily on the Internet. As parents we face tremendous challenges, not least that our children know so much more about the Internet than we do – Chapter 5 considers the obstacles we face as parents and the awareness that we need to cultivate in order to behave responsibly ourselves and bring up trustworthy offspring. Today, those of us using the Internet find ourselves part of online groups, whether it is a family group chat (such as on WhatsApp) or a Facebook group offering the details of our next book club meeting – Chapter 6 looks at this phenomenon and asks how online groups operate, who leads them and the extent to which online groups have become more prominent in our lives than the groups in which we meet face to face. The Internet has an immense potential for doing good in the world, and in Chapter 7 we explore the realm of online volunteering; how from your own home you can reach out to a far-off land to help people you will most probably never meet. We look at the personal fulfillment achieved by the volunteers and some of the outstanding results of their work. Another area where the Internet can really bring about a positive tsunami is in the field of peacemaking between warring factions. We examine how the Internet provides opportunities to improve relations between opposing groups. Finally, in Chapter 8, we examine the future of the Internet, and look deeply at the quality of our own lives in the digital age in which we find ourselves. This chapter also explores what essential steps we can take in order to improve the meaning, the worth, the joy, and the wellbeing in our lives. Throughout, the topics will be organized as a series of questions – ones intended to provoke discussion and inquiry beyond the pages of this book.

A note on pronouns: in the interests of clarity and inclusivity, I have generally favored the third person plural (they) throughout this book. However, in the interest of variation, I sometimes opt for third person singular (he or she). Readers should consider these interchangeable.

WHO ARE WE ONLINE?

"The Internet is an endless opportunity for rebirth."
                                                    – anonymous web surfer

A famous 1993 cartoon in *The New Yorker* shows two dogs, one at a computer keyboard, the other looking at him quizzically. The dog at the computer remarks, "On the Internet, nobody knows you're a dog." Two decades later, that cartoon still expresses the enormous power of the anonymity that the web brings. In fact, many web surfers feel that on the Internet you can do and say whatever you want, no holds barred.

The offline world confronts us with various expectations, labels, and stereotypes that shape us, lay down expectations for us, and influence our behavior. Even if we try to behave outside of the norm, the power of these built-in pressures will often push us back into our old behavior. However, the Internet often presents an alternative – an open window of opportunity for creating a unique identity, a new self, an extreme personal redefinition or a depiction of the person we would like to be.

This chapter will be answering the question: What is it about the online environment that makes it unique?

In order to consider the nature of the Internet's power in creating a unique psychological space, I have broken it down into seven factors:

1. Feeling of anonymity
2. Control over level of physical exposure
3. High control over communications
4. Ease in locating like-minded people
5. Accessibility and availability at all times and places
6. Feeling of equality
7. Fun of web surfing.

Those special advantages, in combination, will crop up not only in this chapter, but all over this book. We'll call them the Magnificent Seven. So, let's start by understanding how the Magnificent Seven influence us as we surf the web (Amichai-Hamburger, 2013).

FEELING OF ANONYMITY

Anonymity means that people hide their real identity from others. Think about Batman disguising his super abilities, pretending in his daily life to be Bruce Wayne, a US billionaire and philanthropist. If you think about it, many of the superheroes wear a mask, which becomes a symbol of the transformation of power from weak to superhuman.

CHATROOM: THE PARTY

Imagine you're at a magnificent costume party, with hundreds of men and women. Everyone is wearing a mask. You wander through the room, and after a while you're addressed by a chubby man with a little goatee. He'd like to speak with you, and he invites you over to the bar across the room. As you walk over, you can't help but wonder about the man behind the mask. You're not even sure of the little that's visible. Is he really chubby? Is the goatee real? Is he even really a male? And what of yourself? You appear to be a heavily made-up elderly woman with blond curls and huge eyeglasses. But just as you can't tell what the man looks like unmasked, he can't be sure how you really look. So why did he pick you out? For the appearance you chose to present? Or maybe because of the uncertainty surrounding the person behind your mask?

A dramatic, mysterious costume party is an example of how anonymity creates an exciting environment that is full of mystery. The influence of masks and costumes to hide behind is liberating for most people, enabling them to depart from their usual behavior. How do we behave when we're masked? Are we unmannerly? Irritable? Passionate? It's a complicated question, and the answer depends on many factors: character, personality, needs, desires, and motivations at the particular time, the nature of the occasion, and the occasion's own rules of behavior. What's forbidden? What's permissible? What's advised?

The feeling in cyberspace is akin to the atmosphere at that costume party, but with many more participants, and an added extra – the option of seeking out for ourselves the particular madcap party we want to attend, or invent. In general, when we're anonymous – in a chat, in a fantasy game, or on a talkback page – we permit ourselves behavior that's more liberated (although within reason, as presumably we do respect the rules of the website).

This liberated behavior sometimes spills over into corners of the Internet where we are meant to be identifiable, such as Facebook. Social networks post rules that forbid the creation of fictitious profiles, but although the rule may be outwardly clear and explicit, some people do create such profiles for the sake of exposure and attention, or for the satisfaction of fooling others (whom they may or may not know). Some phony profiles represent a well-known or even fictitious figure, whom few would believe is really behind the profile – such as SpongeBob SquarePants or Spiderman. But others attempt deceptions that are far more sophisticated such that the deception is unlikely ever to be exposed.

It's important to realize that the web surfer's concept of anonymity is *subjective*. On many sites, visitors may think they're anonymous while the webmaster knows who they are. However, provided that they remain unaware of this fact and continue to believe in their anonymity, their behavior will reflect this, which is to say, it may be different from the kind of activities that would be in evidence if they suspected that they might be identified. In fact, the line between what is anonymous and remains so, and what is merely an illusion of anonymity, is actually very fragile. For example, people might post revealing photos of themselves on a website they consider private and safe, whereas other people wouldn't risk the chance that their friends and relatives might stumble across that website; as we all know, you need only one person to find a photograph and distribute it to understand just how vulnerable we are and how little control we actually have.

CONTROL OVER LEVEL OF PHYSICAL EXPOSURE

On many websites, including most of the text-based chat pages, your physical details aren't visible. It is worth taking some time to consider why this is significant.

Our physical appearance, or to be precise our body image, impacts our self-esteem. Body image, in the modern world, is strongly influenced by messages from the media, which ceaselessly tell us how the ideal man or woman should look. Constant exposure to these types of message has made many people feel very negatively about their appearance; they consider themselves unattractive because they are overweight, underweight, too tall, too short, too dark-skinned, or too pale. This negative body image often leads to low self-esteem (Grilo et al., 1994) and affects every meeting between the individual and the social environment. Enter the Internet, and these same people can unlock themselves from their bodies, leave the prison of their physical appearance, and present themselves in any way they choose. This may lead web surfers to become more confident, more loquacious, or funnier. It may lead them to try to pass themselves off as younger than they are, or more physically attractive – a fantasy version of themselves.

Fantasy environments on the web are places where people choose who they'll pretend to be and what body they'll adopt for themselves in order to express themselves freely.

Even on social networks, people do not necessarily reveal themselves exactly as they appear offline. Many people invest a great deal of time and effort into building an idealized profile, since they are very concerned about how others perceive them. One clear example is found in profile pictures. These form an important part of the personal message the user wishes to transmit. Despite the intention of many web users to present themselves as unique and unusual, profile pictures often form a predictable pattern: boys are photographed at the pool, half in the water, with their muscular arms "casually" flexing on the pool's edge; girls are typically ecstatically happy, in a summertime evening dress and high heels. In keeping with their concern regarding how they are perceived by others, people choose to display what they believe to be their most flattering images, particularly those which hide unflattering parts of themselves. For example, a man who believes he's too fat will post only those pictures that don't expose his "shame" – he'll suck in his stomach, or try to, and take a photo from an angle that doesn't reveal his weight. It isn't surprising, then, that should you meet up with your online acquaintances in an offline setting, you may well fail to recognize quite a few of them.

HIGH CONTROL OVER COMMUNICATIONS

The Internet medium gives us control over communications between ourselves and social contacts, and over the content of the messages we'd like to make known. When we write an e-mail message or update our profile on a social network, we give careful consideration to how we wish to be perceived, and what image we wish to present. We strongly control our image and the messages we prepare – and this ability to revise and so control our response contrasts with the instantaneous response required by a face-to-face meeting or a phone call. In fact, because we choose when to respond, we also choose the environment from which we respond: we tell ourselves, "I'll reply to that over cappuccino, when I'm out of the office and more relaxed."

On the Internet, we are in our own territory, we feel we can break off from communications whenever we want. Think about an online date versus a date in person: Imagine that, in everyday offline life, you're a man who has come to a café to meet someone you thought must be perfect, but instead you find that this person is light-years apart from the description you received. You have nothing in common, and the date is peppered with awkward silences. So what do you do? Presumably you stay there drinking coffee and chit-chatting, until a decent amount of time has passed, or you may even feel forced to invent an "emergency" in order to leave. On the Internet, there are no such unpleasantries. It's quite unlikely you will delay in cutting off a connection once you've determined that you're not meant for each other. Just as people decide quickly whether or not they want to stay on a website, they employ the same tactics at an online date. However, there is a caveat to this: studies of online dating have shown that most people permit themselves to open up more quickly in conversation online than offline. This happens, paradoxically, for the very same reason that the Internet enables you to easily wave the other person away. So, in fact, your online date may be less likely to be comprised of the boring, artificial social niceties that made you run way from the face-to-face encounter, because online people "get real," or at least seem to, more quickly. Chapter 3, which focuses on romantic relationships, has more to say about that.

EASE IN LOCATING LIKE-MINDED PEOPLE

Suppose you live in Minnesota and you like pro soccer. In fact, you're a fan of the San Jose Earthquakes. How near zero are the chances you'll run into a fellow fan anywhere close by? But the Internet is a different kettle of fish. On the web there are hundreds of millions of users, and in addition there's the technology to efficiently, systematically find individuals and groups that resemble ourselves. Suddenly you can find fellow fans and hobbyists organized into groups – called *affinity groups* – for the weirdest, most unusual pursuits. When you find the right group, there are likely to be participants there who will quickly become an important part of your life.

CHATROOM: THE MOOMIN FAN CLUB

When I was a little boy I really enjoyed reading the Moomin series of books by Tove Jansson. The stories are set in Moomin Valley, a beautiful place characterized by a Scandinavian climate with strong winters. The Moomin stories concern eccentric and oddly-shaped characters, some of whom are related to each other. The main characters are MoominPapa, Moominmamma, and Moomintroll. They are loving, and harmonious creatures, full of good intentions. In the first book I read, the other Moomins are all fast asleep when Moomintroll wakes and finds it is midwinter. I remember that, as a child in sunny Israel, I was amazed by this fantastic story, and so I fell in love with the Moomins. In my Internet psychology classes, I used to ask my students if there were any other Moomin fans among us. Often finding myself alone, I would explain to the students that this was no surprise to me, as I had few expectations of finding similar individuals close to home, but should I take a look online, I would surely have no difficulty locating other Moomin fans. When I eventually did go online and take a look, lo and behold, I found a whole plethora of Moomin fan clubs. Immediately I felt my self-esteem bolstered: I was normal; I was no longer alone. Finding similar individuals who enjoy a hobby that is important to you, particularly when others around you are deeply uninterested, is very significant as a symbol of belonging and self-esteem.

Once you have found like-minded people, you may choose to build an affinity group targeting any goal that's important to you. It could be a fight against anti-Semitism, a struggle to save an endangered whale species in the Atlantic, or a campaign to put sassafras back into root beer. Sometimes one spark of enthusiasm is all that's needed for the formation and mobilization of a group. The ease of finding affinity groups can be of great significance to those reluctant to make themselves conspicuous offline. For such people, the Internet can represent a deliverance from frustration and loneliness; they may be people who, for example, have a medical condition that few know about, or hold a minority opinion, or carry some other social stigma. Studies indicate that activities in an affinity group have a very positive influence on the group members' view of themselves (Bargh & McKenna, 2004). After having felt ostracized and isolated, they suddenly discover that there are others like them. They form ties and they understand they're not alone. This communication frequently gives people increased psychological strength, which can often be useful offline as well.

ACCESSIBILITY AND AVAILABILITY AT ALL TIMES AND PLACES

Today, in the age of web surfing by laptop, tablet, and especially the smartphone, the Internet is available everywhere. There is an international research project, of which I am a member, called the World Internet Project (http://worldinternetproject.net); for many years our standard questionnaire would include the following question: "When are you online?" Gradually it dawned on us that this question was no longer relevant, as people have progressed from the desktop computer to the mobile computer, tablet, and smartphone, and that today people are constantly online. In fact, a more appropriate question would be, "When are you offline?" Since Internet connection is now ubiquitous, people surf the web as they converse, as they travel, as they watch TV, even in the bathroom. The Internet really is the city that never sleeps – something is always happening. The news sites bombard us with updates, the forums are full of ideas and announcements, and the members of social networks are ceaselessly adding pictures, clips, likes, and new apps. This never-ending web activity frequently makes us feel that we are missing out if, for any reason, we have not checked one of our regular sites for even a short while, perhaps just a few minutes: Did something happen while we weren't there? Could we have lost prestige because we weren't involved in what was going on? We feel that our identity has weakened, and that we should have been online all the time.

The omnipresent availability of the Internet gives a huge advantage to web-based affinity groups over traditional offline groups. In the past, web-based groups were criticized as lacking significance, since they couldn't compete with "real" groups that brought people together face to face. Today, it seems that the tables have turned and the web-based groups wield more significance than the offline groups. Face-to-face groups require people to plan, schedule, and arrive just to see one another once a week or once a month, and in between meetings nothing much happens. An online group is accessible all the time, and you don't need to go to attend; it's there, wherever you are.

FEELINGS OF EQUALITY

Since its first days, the Internet has been considered an arena of equality. Many believe that teamwork and the feeling of togetherness were what brought about the "big bang" of the Internet as an egalitarian medium (Amichai-Hamburger, 2008). This idea was strengthened by the emergence of the Web 2.0 philosophy (also known as Web2), which emphasizes an experience defined by content generated by users, ease of use, and interactive content (Pierson, Mante-Meijer, & Loos, 2011). With such a philosophy, it should come as no surprise that people feel that, online, everyone can express an opinion; and, in fact, there are a variety of easy to manage tools with which to create such an experience, including blogs, forums, talkbacks, video-sharing sites like YouTube, and social networks such as Facebook. Take for example Amazon, the world's biggest bookstore. On Amazon, a user considering a particular book can see what other books the buyers of that book bought, and can see books recommended on the basis of the user's own previous purchases. In this egalitarian age, your own opinion of a book is as useful and valid as the opinion of a professional critic. Via online reviews, everyone is invited to express an opinion about the book and to share it with the world, and the pattern of opinions will influence the book's future sales. Another example is talkbacks, in which surfers feel free to respond, as they wish, to articles that appear on the web. That freedom may sometimes bring great frustration to the writer of the article, who can suddenly find him or herself extensively criticized by ill-informed readers via talkbacks, but for many people this is an essential part of the web's egalitarian character.

The Internet can provide a way of giving voice to oppressed minorities whose voices are often obliterated by authoritarian regimes. Consider, for example, the shaved-head protest in Iran in Spring 2014, when dozens of Iranian men and women cut off all their hair and posted their pictures online. These pictures were part of a campaign to highlight the abuse of prisoners in one of Iran's notorious prisons, where prison guards had shaved the heads of some political prisoners in order to humiliate them. Many of these prisoners were also beaten. Activists both inside and outside of Iran posted their shaved-head photos on a Facebook page entitled "With the Political Prisoners of Evin's Section 350," using the Persian hashtag *sarfaraz*, or "proud," to promote their campaign. The subsequent removal of the head of Iran's prisons points to the effectiveness of the online action. It gave a platform to the voice of a movement that was unlikely to have been heard in any other way. This freedom of access to a worldwide audience is perhaps the ultimate way to promote true egalitarianism.

By enabling surfers to express themselves, numerous websites turn people from content consumers to actual content creators. This change illustrates the degree of power that each of us receives from the web. An example of how we're creators of content is YouTube, where video clips are shared. We continually hear of success stories that started on

YouTube, including that of superstar Justin Bieber: a young boy who wrote a song, performed it on YouTube, received millions of views, and became a global sensation. Other examples are sites that are created by youngsters and draw thousands of visitors in their first month online. Such instances give the impression that anyone can be the Internet's next meteoric success regardless of age, gender, or origins. Innumerable people are spurred to create content and join in according to the philosophy that "I am the media." Remembering such additional factors as anonymity and lack of physical exposure on the Internet, we can see how the influence of traditional status symbols has been in decline as the feeling of egalitarianism grows stronger. On the Internet, many people feel that if you don't provide the information, nobody knows what clothes you're wearing, what car you drive, or where you live. The Internet is viewed as a place where you can create your own standing regardless of your offline socioeconomic status.

FUN OF WEB SURFING

Surfing the net is enjoyable. As websites compete for the public's interest, time, and money, the result is a growing investment in improving the user experience. Website owners know that they must grab the user within a few seconds or likely lose them permanently. For that reason, sites make an effort to help users quickly and easily master the tools that the site provides and enjoy its various activities and services.

Web surfing is a rapid, fast-paced experience which seems to be constantly accelerating, demanding our attention in many different foci: ads appear flashing round the text we are trying to read, the arrival of a new message is heralded with a ping, news headlines rush across the page. Never before has the human brain been exposed to such rapid-fire input that is in constant flux.

CHATROOM: MY UBER EXPERIENCE

I started using the online transportation service Uber in the summer of 2015 when I was visiting New York. The first time I opened the app to summon a taxi, a message popped up on the screen: Would you like a black car? I did not know or care, but my wife Debbie, a native of London, jumped at the idea of riding in a British black cab in the middle of New York (!), and leaned over to push the "YES" on my phone. It was tremendously exciting to watch the car's progress towards us on my Smartphone – something akin to the marauders map in the Harry Potter books. But when the vehicle arrived, I realized that it was a limo! My wife reminded me that we were running late and couldn't turn back now; however, I was a bit worried about the price so I asked the driver. He said that he would only know the price at the end of the drive – after all, we were talking about rush hour in New York City. We crawled along at a snail's pace with frequent stops and starts, and when finally we reached our destination, I was presented with a sizable bill way beyond what we had intended to spend. There didn't seem anything to be done, not even to negotiate, because after all Uber receives its payment through the credit card it keeps on file. I knew I wouldn't get the money back, and the procedure involved in filing a complaint would be one giant headache, but, on the other hand, I figured expressing my disappointment with their service might at least do something for my blood pressure. So I sent a complaint message. Within five minutes I had a reply: yes, I was in the right, and yes, I should have received some kind of estimate from the driver, and yes, here was a refund of 20 dollars. Like any online experience that wishes to compete in the market, the Uber site deployed a combination of digital intervention, human understanding, and fast response time in order to successfully compete for my patronage.

WHERE DOES THIS ALL LEAD?

Now that we have outlined the power of the Internet by way of the Magnificent Seven – Feeling of anonymity; Control over level of physical exposure; High control over communications; Ease in locating like-minded people; Accessibility and availability at all times and places; Feeling of equality; Fun of web surfing – we can consider their effects. Altogether, the Internet has created an amazing environment, one in which people are empowered psychologically in the most amazing ways, and which has an impact on many spheres of their lives. These include feelings of being protected, the ability to recreate oneself endlessly, and opportunities to develop interests and find similar others. This is particularly true for people who cannot easily find similar others in their immediate surroundings. Feeling protected also creates an expansion of the omnipotent self and opens a way to enrich our identity in many new directions, some of which we wouldn't have had the courage to explore outside of the Internet, and some of which may not have existed, or would have been harder to do, before the advent of the Internet.

This empowerment may be particularly exciting for the many autodidacts, who may now become members of esoteric discussion groups in contexts where their lack of formal education is not a hindrance. Doing so helps them also to change their own definition and sometimes may encourage them to seek more formal knowledge in this direction.

People may also feel they can reach a higher level of efficiency as a result of being in several places at the same time. They feel that they can know everything, see everything, and be everywhere. A few years ago, this would have sounded like science fiction, but this is now our reality. In a mere five minutes, you could watch a video on a future vacation in Finland, be involved in a discussion on the application of humanism in daily life, post a new funny photo on Facebook, and enjoy the subsequent social interaction with your friends when they write humorous comments on your post. The ease of access to information creates the feeling that you have all the information you need with you all the time. This means that you are able to challenge formal authorities. So if, for example, you are in a lecture you can check whether what the professor just quoted was correct, or – in what has increasingly become a norm – check a few sites and challenge your doctor's medical advice. Altogether, a great sense of empowerment has been created.

The endless outlets for sharing information with others – be it a photo on Instagram, a video on YouTube, or even the ability to start a blog – encourages people to express themselves in many creative ways that we did not know in the past. People nowadays believe the expression, "I'm the *media*." You are no longer a mere consumer of media, but rather a provider of media.

One amazing example of the psychological empowerment the Internet provides is the many global online volunteering projects whereby people take it upon themselves to help other people, often internationally. One example of such a project is that run by Elizabeth and Tim Rose from Canada (Amichai-Hamburger, 2008). The aim of their work is to improve the lives of homeless children in

Zambia. Elizabeth and Tim, a mother and son who work from home, use the Internet to identify and contact potential donors of sports equipment. For those willing to contribute, they design a mechanism for collecting the donated items and shipping them to Zambia. Can you imagine a child in Zambia, who feels that no one cares about him, suddenly receiving, out of the blue, a gift box filled with amazing sports equipment such as T-shirts, a football whistle, and other great things? This event obviously brings great happiness to the child. The feeling that the world cares brings light to the young one's life, and is likely to bolster his self-esteem. This is an example of how the Internet can empower people so that they can have an impact on the world. What makes Elizabeth and Tim Rose's project even more amazing is the fact that Tim is paraplegic. If Tim conducted face-to-face meetings with sports equipment manufacturers, he may well encounter discrimination and, as a result, his visionary ideas might be ignored. However, using the Internet to approach these manufacturers makes his physical condition irrelevant and he has been listened to and cooperated with. If you think about it, the Internet has helped Tim to become a kind of superman. A person who needs help has become someone who can provide help with a global impact. This is a high level of empowerment. We'll talk more about the power to do good online in Chapter 7.

THE FLIPSIDE: CAN THINGS GO WRONG?

So far we have discussed the positive components of the Internet; in fact, it has been painted as a truly desirable environment, one in which we would all like to dwell. This, however, is not the whole picture, and in fact those very components that give us those positive experiences on the Internet are also those that can turn the whole thing on its head, and ultimately lead people to harm themselves and others. Below, we'll discuss the ways in which the Magnificent Seven – explored in a positive light above – can have a negative effect that is also worthy of consideration.

Feeling of anonymity and control over levels of physical exposure can certainly encourage people to express themselves freely, but that does not mean that they will necessarily do so in a positive, prosocial manner. The very anonymity of the Internet may be the reason why people feel enabled to express themselves violently online. Many people feel reluctant to express aggression offline due to the social retribution this will provoke; however, under the cover and protection of the Internet's anonymity, their inhibitions dissolve. This can cause aggression and anger to be released with no constraints, often with terrifying results.

CHATROOM: MY FIRST ONLINE POST

Some years ago, I published an article on a major website about one of my studies concerning Internet psychology. Since it was the first time I'd written for the mass media, I invested a lot of thought and time in the article, and I was interested in how people would respond. Many of the talkbacks dismayed me: "Who is this moron?" "They should have left this Hamburger on the grill." "Blah, blah, what a retard." And those were just a few of the milder ones! I admit I felt humiliated. I'd just had my first exposure to the realm of talkbacks, and I needed time before I understood that it wasn't necessarily personal. For some people, the comments section is a sparring ring and the harder they punch, the better they feel about themselves. It just so happened that, by publishing my article, I had positioned myself to take the punches.

In terms of the negatives, *high control over physical exposure* and *high control over communications* go hand-in-hand. The ability to modify the message constantly can very easily become an obsession. People may become fixated on creating the *perfect* message that presents them as their ideal. This underlines a major difference between messages that are part of the online chit-chat, where people are usually carefree and uninhibited, and those communications when we are particularly aware of the impression we wish to create. We witness this on sites like Facebook, when people often take an inordinate amount of time crafting a post or photograph.

It is important to be aware that these feelings of control are often an illusion. And it is this mistaken feeling of control that leads people to be too open with the information they provide on the net, which in some cases may harm them.

While *ease in finding like-minded people* may certainly be a blessing for many people, the results will clearly depend on the inclinations of the seeker. It is true that many people seek a group with which they can better the world or share a safe, enjoyable, and often innocuous hobby; however, there are many who will use this facility to find others with the same harmful, damaging tendencies. In other words, the ease with which one person finds others who are excited by quilt-making is the same as that with which another will find others similarly interested in bullying a colleague or bomb-making. This, together with the protection, reinforcement, and constant availability of their online associates, can lead to horrendous results.

Accessibility and availability at all times and places has created a situation in which there is no longer a separation between work time and leisure time (or, indeed, time off). When it comes to work, you are expected to be constantly available, even during a lunch break away from the workplace or, worse, when on vacation. Many people are continually working: at all times of the day and night, and from any and every location. The lack of time or place to unwind, relax, and switch-off has a significant and negative impact on our well-being.

CHATROOM: VACATION IN BORA BORA

John was very proud of himself: after seven years as a junior partner in a law firm in Dallas he had succeeded in saving enough money for a great vacation in Bora Bora with his partner, Melissa. Bora Bora is located in the South Pacific; US news outlets tend to bill the destination as "the best island in the world." John planned a week-long vacation in a bungalow on the water, part of the fabulous Four Seasons Resort featuring amazing accommodation and dining in a very intimate atmosphere. This was going to be a memorable vacation for him and Melissa. They had anticipated it for so long, especially during the last year when John had been immersed in a major deal for a clients and had been working round the clock; he'd spent hardly any time away from his mobile phone, with its constant flow of emails and text messages. Now the moment they'd waited for had arrived, and they watched from the plane as Bora Bora came into view with its clean sandy beaches, crystal-clear water, and huge palm trees. They were arriving in a paradise on earth! As they walked into the lobby of the hotel, John's mobile rang. He was sure it was his mother, who was looking after their child. Unfortunately, however, it was the office. There was a crisis and his boss needed John to go over some documents. She'd send them immediately. As John and Melissa entered the hotel lobby, the receptionist greeted them with a warm, welcoming smile.

John responded to her by asking for the hotel's WiFi code. This was actually the beginning and the end of the vacation. The crisis was bigger than first thought and while John was physically in Bora Bora, mentally he was at the office. Melissa tried to be understanding, but she was very disappointed and upset. John finished the "vacation" exhausted.

One perhaps unforeseen effect of *feeling of equality* on the Internet is that many net users, particularly younger ones, may feel their social status is unstable and that they must thus constantly prove their self-worth. Every post or photo they put up is part of the social exam that they are continuously submitting themselves to. To pass the exam they need a high result of likes, comments, and shares for each post. People even develop a variety of strategies to pass this exam. If the result isn't good, that is, they do not get a satisfactory response, they might prefer to remove their post rather than display their "failure."

While the *fun of surfing the web* is undeniable, this fun can lead very easily to addiction. User experience is the name of the game on the Internet, and it guarantees that Internet experiences will only become more engaging and pleasurable in the future. As a result, it is likely we will see more and more individuals being addicted to the net. Nowadays, we know of many different kinds of online addiction, from games and gambling to pornography.

When considering the causes of net addiction, it's important to bear in mind that some people find it difficult to function socially in an offline environment; the more positively enhanced their web experience becomes, the more potentially challenging they may find facing the world beyond the Internet. For many, the Internet may begin to shift from their preferred reality to their only reality.

CHATROOM: LIVING ON THE NET

Ben was a 17-year-old boy who'd been identified as an exceptionally clever child at a very young age. He was so smart that he was an undergraduate by the age of 16. However, although he was cognitively brilliant, Ben's social abilities were very poor and, as a result, he was very isolated. The few people he interacted with treated him not as a friend or peer but as a help desk to go to when they needed assistance with math problems or computers, the subjects Ben studied at the university. They had long since stopped initiating small talk with him or inviting him to any social events. However, while he was very lonely offline, on the Internet Ben had a completely different social life. He was heavily involved in a particular game and had become a central member of its community of players. His parents were concerned that he didn't do anything else, and indeed he often skipped meals and, on some occasions, hardly slept. He even started missing university classes because he couldn't wake up in the morning if he'd been gaming all night. His parents tried to persuade him to see an addiction therapist, but he was resistant. As he said, "This is my fun in life. This is where I'm most alive. Why should I give up on that?" Finally, however, Ben recognized the price of his "fun" and started working on his recovery. He has a long way to go.

It is clear that each of the seven factors that can empower net users can also have an inverse effect – one that is negative or dangerous.

A FINAL WORD

The Internet is a powerful psychological environment with great potential to empower the user. However, whether its use has a positive or negative outcome depends on the person using it – their tendencies and goals. We have to bear in mind that the Internet is a form of technology, and, like any technology, it is not inherently good or bad; rather, it has the potential to be used for both. This calls for a need to be highly aware of the challenges presented by the Internet.

REFERENCES

Amichai-Hamburger, Y. (2008). Potential and promise of online volunteering. *Computers in Human Behavior*, 24, 544–562.

Amichai-Hamburger, Y. (2013). Reducing intergroup conflict in the digital age. In H. Giles (Ed.), *The Handbook of Intergroup Communication* (pp. 181–193). New York: Routledge.

Bargh, J., & McKenna, K. A. (2004). The Internet and social life. *Annual Review of Psychology*, 55, 573–590.

Grilo, C. M., Wilfley, D. E., Brownell, K. D., & Rodin, J. (1994). Teasing, body image, and self-esteem in a clinical sample of obese women. *Addictive Behaviors*, 19, 443–450.

Pierson, J., Mante-Meijer, E. A., & Loos, E. F. (2011). *New Media Technologies and User Empowerment*. Berlin: Peter Lang.

2

DOES OUR PERSONALITY AFFECT OUR ONLINE BEHAVIOR?

"My personality relocated to the Internet a long time ago."
— anonymous web surfer

In this chapter we will be asking an encompassing question: Does our personality affect our behavior online? In addition, we will be looking at the extent to which we use the Internet as an environment to express our uninhibited needs. We will delve into the realm of online therapy: How does it actually work? What would the famous psychologist Sigmund Freud think about it? We will also be discussing what kind of personalities gain most from the Internet, and the relevance of some leading personality theories in psychology to the Internet.

Within the field of psychology, the sub-field of the psychology of personality is unique in that it sees the individual as one integrative unit. It is an interesting contrast to most other areas of psychology, which explore specific aspects of human behavior, such as perception or memory. Personality represents "those characteristics of the person that account for his pattern of behavior" (Pervin, 1993: 3). Thus, in this schema, each of us has a specific personality that is responsible for our consistent behavioral patterns. In our own lives, we rely on certain assessments; for example, we may look at a man and say he is the kind of guy who is open to new experiences and gets excited about events in his daily life. We may look at someone else and say she is very quiet and shy; someone who doesn't like to be surrounded by many people. As individuals, we do this kind of profiling all the time, often instantaneously and unconsciously, because it helps us to understand people. In other words, we are constantly attempting to define people's personality.

The question we wish to consider – "What does psychology have to do with the Internet?" – requires that we first demonstrate how personality, the basic building block of psychology, relates to what we do on the Internet. One way to do this is to try to second-guess how the fathers of present-day psychology, such as Sigmund Freud, Carl Jung and Carl Rogers, who attempted to define our personality and development, would have answered this question. Since it is almost impossible to talk about Freud, the founding father of analysis, without talking about therapy, we will be taking a look at the growing field of therapy through the net, i.e., online therapy.

FREUD AND THE INTERNET: CAN THE INTERNET ACCOMMODATE THE TOPPLING OF CONVENTIONS AND RELEASE OF THE ID?

Sigmund Freud is considered to be the founder of modern psychology. His great contribution is not only in understanding the mind, but also in forming an approach to therapy for people whose minds are suffering – that is, psychoanalysis. This approach links the patient's reported symptoms to an emotional and mental stalling, or *fixation*, in early childhood. The trained therapist helps the patient, by means of a long and structured process, to revisit an early stage and handle the fixation. Freud's theories became the basis for the study of psychology. Although many of his followers later parted ways with him, and other leading psychologists have disagreed with elements of his theories, his contribution to our understanding of the human mind was enormous. I myself am among those who don't accept his theories word for word, but I am full of appreciation for Freud as the pioneer who shaped modern psychology.

An interesting question related to Freud has to do with the way in which people express themselves on the net. We find that in many Internet arenas, especially those that maintain people's anonymity, some individuals express themselves very explicitly, through violent or sexual messages. Does such behavior reflect a true expression of what Freud called the "id," that is, the basic, instinctual drives of the human being?

SIGMUND FREUD, THE FATHER OF PSYCHOLOGY

Sigmund Freud (1856–1939) was a neurologist and psychologist. A Viennese Jew by birth, he laid the foundations for understanding human personality by creating a theoretical and therapeutic approach called psychoanalysis (*psyche* is a Greek word describing the soul or mind) in which the human mind is the target of investigation. Below are some principal points from his rich and complex theory.

Imagine a giant iceberg afloat in the arctic. How would you describe it? Probably you'd mention the impressive mountain of visible ice above the waterline, but would you remember that most of the iceberg is underwater? According to Freud, the human personality is built like an iceberg: it has parts that are visible, but also large parts we are unaware of. Freud would say that the critical mass of personality resides in the region of unawareness, the invisible region. This unknown mass, the unconscious, is the dominant influence in our lives.

Freud's theory attributes great significance to the first years of our lives. As we pass through the developmental stages from birth to the age of six, we gradually gain familiarity with the various areas of our body. If a baby's needs aren't sufficiently addressed at a particular stage, or get too much attention, that person's psychological development will be affected. In this way, people's early childhood pursues them throughout their lives.

Freud presents the human personality as composed of three parts: the id, the ego, and the superego. The *id* is impatient for gratification; it says, "I want it all here and now." Deep in the id, uncontrollable urges for sex and destruction seek to come forth. The *ego* tries to moderate the id's urges and allow the id some form of expression that accommodates the reality of society's accepted laws and principles. If the ego didn't moderate people's brute urges, their destructiveness and unbridled sexuality would land them in prison.

> The *superego* represents society's values and its firm moral codes, internalized by people who receive them from parents, from teachers, and from other agents of society.
>
> Thus humans face daily competition from the id, which calls from the unconscious for total release, the superego which wants to shove the id back into the unconscious, and the ego which mediates between them and tries to grant the id some socially legitimate expression.

Even the Internet has its rules. You may notice them as soon as you land on the home page of a site that is open for public use. A public website posts regulations notifying every visitor of the behavior that is expected and what behaviors violate the rules of conduct for the site. Repeated violations may result in a "ban" against the "offender." A forum lays down clear rules such as "Keep your language clean," "Don't start a battle of insults," "Direct any complaints against participants to the forum administrators," or "No sale of illegal or stolen merchandise." The penalty is clear: "Violators will be blocked." If you are on Facebook and you use extremely aggressive language with some of your "friends," they are liable to remove you from their list of contacts and perhaps even to block you from viewing their personal page. If you belong to a group of people where aggressive language is used against some third party (a celebrity you hate, for example), you might be able to express your violence, but should you become extremely violent or threatening, the administrators of the social network may well close the group. But to what extent are these rules implemented? Theoretically, each Facebook user has agreed to adhere to the following regulations:

1. You will not bully, intimidate, or harass any user.
2. You will not post content that: is hate speech, threatening, or pornographic; incites violence; or contains nudity or graphic or gratuitous violence.

However, in reality, Facebook does little to reinforce those rules for the simple reason that it plays against its best interest, which is maximum traffic. Through ad sales, Facebook has found a way to monetize traffic on the site. Emotions and excitement result in more people joining in on the discussion, which ultimately creates more profit for Facebook. Therefore, the administrators of Facebook want to keep control of their own censorship policy, and would not welcome external censorship, which they believe would damage their image significantly. It is much better for their PR to use exalted language, declaiming the decency and high standards maintained by Facebook, despite the reality that the site plays host to a large number of hate groups that call on their members to commit acts of violence. It is exceptionally rare to get Facebook to shut down a hate group, and it does so only after a considerable amount of outside pressure.

In general, most users behave in a respectful way online, but some people lose control on the Internet in what seems to represent, at least partly, instances of the id overpowering the ego, and with it, all that is logical and rational. Freud stressed the human need to regress, which he saw as a repetitive compulsion toward self-destruction (what he called the "death instinct"). We can see this type of behavior playing out in different online addictions, be it to games, gambling, or pornography, where the person feels that he has to repeatedly return to a specific behavior, despite the fact that it is irrational and interferes with normal functioning. However, we have to be cautious in our conclusions because sometimes the most ridiculous behavior, online or elsewhere, might actually represent a regression that is not irrational, but rather is a *regression in the service of the ego*. That is to say, acting immaturely may in some cases advance the ego's long-term goals. Such a possibility was defined by followers of Freud who extended the power of the ego in their personality theory. In other words, while some people are able to take positive experiences from their past to strengthen their ability to cope effectively in the present, it may be that others seek to overcome the negative experiences of their past by replaying such experiences again and again in the present, ultimately revising them so that they have a more positive interpretation. Some people do this through the use of a fantasy environment on the Internet, where they adopt various identities and replay past experiences in ways that will strengthen their ability to cope with the challenges they face in their present life.

E-THERAPY: HOW DOES IT WORK, IS IT A GOOD IDEA, AND WHAT WOULD FREUD THINK?

One of the most amazing psychological developments on the net is online therapy, also known as e-therapy. This has been defined in various ways. One of the more comprehensive definitions is as follows: "a licensed mental health care professional providing mental health services via email, video conferencing, virtual reality technology, chat technology, or any combination of these" (Manhal-Baugus, 2001: 551).

PROS AND CONS OF E-THERAPY

There are great advantages to e-therapy. In the offline world, many people are frightened of signing on for therapy because of the social stigma surrounding mental health issues. They are fearful that should it be known they are receiving counseling – suppose they meet someone they know on the way to the therapist's office or even at the bus stop – then they would be labeled as having issues and thus become a social outcast. In the online world, there is no fear of being stigmatized: you won't be seen entering a clinic and you don't even leave the house. For many people, the Internet is perceived as a safer, more secure environment than the offline world (Amichai-Hamburger & Hayat, 2013; Hamburger & Ben-Artzi, 2000), and they are therefore much more likely to find the courage to undertake e-therapy. The Internet also solves the logistical issue of transportation to the therapist, which is a relevant concern for a range of individuals. For people living in outlying areas, or for people with mobility issues, the challenge of actually getting to a therapist is huge, and the availability of therapy in their own home can be a pivotal factor in their ability to obtain therapy. There is also the cost; therapy itself may well be expensive on- and offline, but for some, the cost of traveling may make it prohibitively expensive. Online therapy may also reduce waiting times (Wright et al., 2005).

It is not only those who live in remote places who may have difficulty finding a therapist – people living in more central locations may nonetheless find locating a therapist who fits their own needs, both personal and cultural, challenging. The Internet provides tremendous scope and opportunity to find the right fit. The Internet also enables patients from a minority culture to find a therapist who shares their cultural or religious beliefs, even if that therapist is located physically in another state or even another country. A colleague of mine, a psychiatrist and online therapist living in Tel Aviv, has several patients in Los Angeles. These patients – all Israelis who prefer to work with an Israeli, Hebrew-speaking therapist – found my colleague online. Today, for those who relocate or travel frequently for work, technology allows their therapy to continue with the same person (Wright et al., 2005).

Like regular therapy, the Internet sets up a therapeutic relationship between the patient and therapist; online therapy accommodates the various approaches that are relevant in the field today. Sessions are held using various means of communication, from private, text-only chat to video-chatting applications like Skype that make the patient and therapist visible to each other. The secure online environment is also likely to aid in the creation of a therapeutic relationship online.

Online therapy has proved successful in treating a variety of problems, ranging from eating disorders, depression, and addictions (e.g., nicotine, alcohol, gambling) to various forms of anxiety that harm a person's functioning by generating tension and unease.

In situations in which the patient becomes a potential danger to him or herself or to the surroundings, or when a deterioration occurs in their condition that leads to difficulties in everyday functioning, clearly the Internet cannot take the place of face-to-face treatment that is absolutely essential. It can, however, function as a first-step resource and a connection point with professionals, enabling the patient to rally and report for therapy in person. Such cases could involve, for example, severe depression or psychosis (where the patient loses touch with reality and hallucinates), or bipolar disorder ("manic-depression," whereby the individual swings between deep depression and extreme euphoria).

However, e-therapy has also received intense backlash. Here, we will discuss some of the main criticisms leveled against it. In comparison with traditional therapy, in which the patient knows the identity of the therapist, in online therapy this may not be true. Such a criticism suggests that the entire realm of e-therapy is an unprofessional, irresponsible method. However, this is in fact unfair as the therapist and any information given about him or her can be examined and verified. Yes, there are going to be instances of fraudulent therapists, but this is true in the traditional world of face-to-face therapy too. Another criticism suggests that e-therapy is missing the crucial component of body language, which helps the therapist to read the patient's hidden messages; that is, because in text-based therapy body language is totally invisible, misunderstandings may result. It is true that there are cases in which a patient's body language may express profound distress that they are not articulating verbally, and which would not come through in text; in such instances, the e-therapist will not be able to react properly. It is, however, important to stress that, alongside the text-only e-therapy, today a whole range of treatment models exist, including Skype or similar platforms, that allow an interaction using audio and video channels through which the interacting parties are exposed to each other's non-verbal communication. Nevertheless, returning to Freud, I would argue that in fact the text-only e-therapy has components that he would be happy with. After all, in classic Freudian therapy, the patient lies on the couch in order to enter a state of near-sleep that enables the unconscious to express itself, while the therapist sits in a chair at an angle that leaves the patient invisible. The absence of any line of sight between them is intended to help liberate the patient from inner defenses so that he or she may confidently release his or her story. It gives the patient a feeling of disconnection from daily experience, and of undisturbed immersion in their own narrative. In this way, the sheltered situation allows the patient to reconnect to his or her past, which in turn allows the therapist to help undo the emotional binds created in the past. Such a state, it could be argued, would be possible via text-only e-therapy.

A related criticism argues that because of the partial or total lack of nonverbal communication and the geographical distance, a patient's signal of a wish to commit suicide might not be detected, leading to horrific results. This challenge can be dealt with by training therapists to assess suicide risk online, by examining risk and contributing factors as well as warning signs in a manner akin to the process for assessing suicide risk in traditional clinical, face-to-face evaluations (e.g., Posner, Melvin, Stanley, Oquendo, & Gould, 2007). It is important to note that today phone and online crisis hotlines are common practice throughout the world (Witte et al., 2010). Also, e-therapists should work with adequate emergency backup systems in the early stages of treatment with all patients, even if some patients view such backup as irrelevant or unimportant. For those who pose a suicide risk, a safety plan should be put into place (Stanley et al., 2008).

Another criticism suggests that racial, cultural, and ethnic differences between therapist and patient are likely to be greater in the global, diverse online world as compared to traditional psychotherapy, and the therapist consequently might not understand the interaction and come to false conclusions (Sue, 2006). In this case, awareness of the challenge might well prevent falling into such a trap. Before e-therapy starts, the therapist should learn the profile of the patient, including his or her background and culture, and act upon this knowledge during the therapy sessions.

Another criticism points out the technical obstacles, as some patients may not have access to the required equipment, or may be challenged by the digital skills required to be treated through e-therapy. This is clearly valid in some cases, though many people throughout the world are becoming increasingly digitally literate. In addition, high-quality equipment has become more widely available.

IN TREATMENT

Many forms of therapy can now take place online. Here are some of the most common examples.

Psychoanalysis is lengthy in comparison to other treatment models. It focuses on understanding and exposing the unconscious. Psychoanalysis tries to reach the deep, unconscious influences underlying the patient's distress, rather than focusing only on the patient's reported symptoms such as episodes of anxiety or compulsive behavior. Psychoanalysis puts great emphasis on analyzing the relationship between patient and therapist, considering it an important source of information and an avenue for learning about the central figures and relationships in the patient's life.

Integrative cognitive behavioral therapy (iCBT) focuses on the behavioral level of the problem. It teaches the patient to gradually create a healthier model of behavior, replacing troublesome old behavioral patterns. The therapy involves continual support and relevant "homework" from the therapist. This kind of therapy has proven very effective for various forms of anxiety. More information is available at www.online-therapy.com/cbt.

Virtual reality (VR) therapy uses the Internet as a vividly experienced alternative reality. Like cognitive behavioral therapy, VR therapy involves providing the patient with gradual, controlled exposure to the troubling experience. However, unlike the treatments mentioned above, VR does not have to involve a dialogue between the patient and the therapist. This treatment is suitable for a variety of phobias, such as fear of spiders or heights. On the VR platform, a person with claustrophobia, for example – fear of being shut in – can gradually practice various situations in which they appear to be confined: in a large hall, an elevator, and so on.

E-therapy is developing all the time. Initially such therapy used text only; now, however, many e-therapists are using Skype and similar technologies that allow the therapist and patient to see one another. In the future, e-therapists may well be able to use sophisticated software that will analyze the therapy session more fully and come up with some directions for the therapist to explore. For example, the software might detect repetition of metaphors and use of certain words, or specific body movements made in association with specific words. This might lead in turn to specific directions that the therapist would be able to explore and examine. Also in the future, therapists will be able to utilize applications that will help them to analyze the behavior of their patient outside of the therapy session, which will help them to build a more comprehensive understanding of the patient and his or her situation. The therapist will be able to utilize technology to provide the patient with tools that can help them cope with their specific challenges. For example, imagine having an application on a smartphone that measures the heart rate of a patient, thus providing evidence of when and where the patient becomes anxious and nervous. With such technology, the therapist might then be able to work with the patient to analyze what is causing him or her stress, and provide tools to avoid or counter this automatic negative reaction to the specific stimuli, and perhaps even finding a more effective reaction. This ability to continue therapeutic work outside of the confines of a session may well lead to much more successful outcomes.

WHO BENEFITS FROM THE INTERNET?

As explained previously, the Internet's power comes from creating a unique psychological space that offers a combination of advantages available nowhere else in life. In Chapter 1, we termed these advantages the Magnificent Seven: feeling of anonymity; control over level of physical exposure; high control over communications; ease in locating like-minded people; accessibility and availability at all times and places; feeling of equality; and fun of web surfing. With this in mind, let us examine which personality profiles might be best suited to utilizing this unique psychological environment to empower themselves. For example, consider the specific question: Who benefits more from interacting on the Internet? Is it those in social poverty (the introverts) or the socially prosperous (the extroverts)? In the most basic terms, introverts are shy, reticent people; extroverts are outgoing, expressive people. There is a variety of evidence regarding who flourishes more online.

PERSONALITY: ARE YOU AN EXTROVERT OR AN INTROVERT?

You might be interested to learn whether you are an extrovert or an introvert. To get an indication, answer the following questions:

1. Usually I prefer a good book over a party.
   Yes/No
2. I don't feel comfortable at social events.
   Yes/No
3. In social interactions, I let the other side start the conversation.
   Yes/No
4. I'm usually very quiet when I attend social events.
   Yes/No
5. I'm not the person to light up a tired party.
   Yes/No

If you answered all these questions positively, you are probably an introvert; if you answered negatively, you are probably an extrovert. This is obviously only a slight indication of your propensity for either introversion or extraversion. For a better picture, take a look at Eysenck and Eysenck (1975).

Robert Kraut and his team (2002) found that the degree of influence exerted by the Internet depends on the individual being influenced – on whether they are an introvert or an extrovert. For extroverts, the Internet is an additional channel for the social adeptness they delight in. The extrovert brings field-proven social skills from the offline world, wields the same skills online, and thus preserves a social dominance over the introvert. The introvert, on the other hand, remains socially less adept online as well, and has a visibly hard time functioning in social situations and establishing ties, just as in the offline world.

However, in a series of studies I conducted, I showed that the Internet can, contrary to Kraut's conclusions, be a place where *introverts benefit more than extroverts*. In those studies, I found that since introverts have trouble establishing social ties in day-to-day life, they use the Internet as an arena for compensating for their weaknesses, seizing the opportunity to show initiative and assume social leadership. The introverts are not limited by the longstanding socially imposed definitions that burdened them hitherto. They can redefine themselves, be someone who is open and sociable, and succeed in forming important social ties (Amichai-Hamburger & Hayat, 2013).

Such studies support the approach of Carl Jung (see the nearby Mini-biography) and raise the possibility that the special Internet environment may help to produce a balance between introversion and extraversion. The Internet space gives introverts a means of compensating for their difficulties, and allows them to pursue successful social interactions by providing a channel for their hidden extroverted side. It is fascinating to see how activity on the Internet today coincides with Jung's thinking and lends a new perspective to a theory that he first published more than eighty years ago.

MINI-BIOGRAPHY: CARL JUNG, OPPOSITES THAT ADD UP

Carl Gustav Jung (1875–1961) was a leading psychiatric practitioner and lecturer at the University of Zurich. He first encountered the work of Sigmund Freud in 1900, when he read Freud's book, *The Interpretation of Dreams* (1899). The book deeply influenced Jung, and gradually he began to adopt Freud's ideas, which at the time were not accepted in reputable medical circles. In 1906 Jung wrote an article defending Freud's ideas, and as a result Freud invited him to visit in Vienna. After thirteen hours of uninterrupted conversation with Freud, Jung officially became his disciple.

However, after some years as Freud's senior disciple, Jung began to disagree with some of his mentor's ideas. Among the points of disagreement was the central position Freud attributed to repressed sexuality in the unconscious. For his part, Jung introduced new ideas, among them the idea of "cultural archetypes." This refers to a pool of shared human experience that influences people subconsciously and resides in the collective unconscious of the human race, passing from generation to generation. Such ideas were heresy according to Freud, but Jung wasn't swayed from his personal search for truth, nor from adding ideas from a wide range of sources to his theories.

One of the most fascinating influences on Jung was East Asian philosophy, and from there he took the concept of yang and yin. These fundamental opposites are considered a symmetrical pair of forces that combine to make a whole. Among the aspects of personality that Jung considered important are introversion and extraversion. According to Jung, extroverts act in a sociable way, seek the company of others, go looking for excitement and risk, and act on impulse; conversely, introverts are quiet, prefer to stay alone, and may be seen as distant and solitary. Introversion and extraversion, Jung emphasized, aren't essentially in conflict; rather, they should achieve dialogue and reconciliation as an avenue to mental health.

As a researcher in the psychology department at New York University, John Bargh led a research group (Bargh, McKenna, & Fitzsimons, 2002) that examined Carl Rogers' idea of "the real self" in the Internet arena, and they found that some people express themselves better online than offline. Lonely people and people with social anxiety found the Internet environment more comfortable for expressing their "real self" and preferred that environment as a place for making friends, establishing romantic ties, and forming significant relationships for the long term.

In a follow-up study that I conducted with Galit Wainapel and Shaul Fox (2002) of Bar Ilan University, we found similar results to those in Bargh, McKenna, and Fitzsimon's (2002) study: introverted people and neurotic people in general tended to position their "real self" on the Internet; that is, they felt safer about expressing themselves on the web, and they built their significant relationships there.

It's important to understand the significance of those findings. In the US, for example, 15 million people suffer from social anxiety (ADAA, 2007). In other words, our research indicated that a sizable proportion of the population may prefer online life as a refuge; a place of compensation where they can do what the offline world makes difficult for them. To a great extent this finding is still true today, although one must note that when this research took place, most Internet sites were anonymous. It seems, then, that introverts feel that they can open up, express themselves, and form significant relationships online, to a much greater degree than offline. In many regards, the Internet has become the preferred environment for many people's self-expression.

Another online location that offers empowerment to everyone (and especially to introverts) is the community of Wikipedia, the free online encyclopedia (www.wikipedia.com). User-generated, it has become the world's largest encyclopedia. One unique trait of this community is the anonymity of the editors; Wikipedia's readers don't know the identity of the editors. A study into the personalities of Wikipedia editors conducted with my research team (Amichai-Hamburger, Lamdan, Madiel, & Hayat, 2008) found that, overall, they tend to be introverted people who are closed to new experiences and describe the Internet as their preferred environment. The research results indicated that many Wikipedia editors are socially inhibited, and tend to use their Wikipedia anonymity as a way both to compensate for this and to express themselves.

Newer studies also point to a tendency among Wikipedians to be closed and introverted people (Yang & Lai, 2010). That is not to say, of course, that no Wikipedians are extroverts, only that such individuals are exceptions.

MINI-BIOGRAPHY: CARL ROGERS, LOVE WITHOUT LIMITS

Carl Rogers (1902–1987) was a US psychologist, humanist, and romantic. He had a very strict upbringing, and high expectations were placed on him by his demanding parents. Against that complicated back-story, Carl Rogers sought to be heard in a unique personal voice that would eventually find its most central expression in his psychological theory. Rogers' approach can be seen as a total overturning of Freud's: whereas Freud believed that people are inherently bad, Rogers believed that people are essentially good at heart, and that their primary ambition is to actualize their higher capabilities to the maximum. According to Rogers, children receive the message from society and its representatives (namely, parents and teachers) that a certain cultural code of behavior is the only path to acceptance and love, and Rogers blamed that message for the failure of most people to achieve successful self-expression.

The message that love is conditional on a specific ideal of good behavior is what sidetracks people and leads them to abandon their "real self" in favor of behavior that they think will ensure the love of the people around them, whom they care about. Society instills its values into people, and those values turn into an inner voice, apparently objective, telling everyone what they should and should not do.

The ability of introverts to use the Internet as a venue for genuine and essential self-expression, free from certain societal pressures, can be perceived as an attempt to express their real selves.

Chats are another interesting medium. Most chatrooms permit anonymity, and therefore our working assumption would be that they appeal more to introverts than extroverts. Indeed, a research team headed by Luigi Anolli of the University of Milan (Anolli, Villani, & Riva, 2005) found that frequent use of anonymous chatrooms is strongly linked to having an introverted, closed personality. In explaining their findings, the researchers pointed to my report that introverts tend to favor the Internet arena as a place to express themselves and build social connections.

The introvert's fingerprints are visible in another intriguing place: fantasy games. In 2008, when Robert Dunn of the University of Tennessee and Rosanna Guadagno of the University of Alabama researched games in which players choose avatars (virtual characters that represent the players inside the game), they expected the human player's personality to be one factor in the choice. The researchers found that, indeed, introverts invested more in designing the look of their avatars, evidently more concerned than extroverts about making their online representatives appealing.

Thus, the Internet provides opportunities for many people to compensate for what they feel they lack. It has emerged that in the three examples above – Wikipedia, chatrooms, and fantasy games – the introverts proved their ability to compensate for their closed personalities. It seems that such safe places on the Internet are a preferred venue for the self-expression of introverts. In a way, the introverts have made the Internet a kind of paradise where they can fulfill and express themselves, unconstrained by their offline image.

Internet use on the part of introverts is clearly a complex issue. On the one hand, the Internet is clearly useful for introverts and similar others as a safe place for self-expression; on the other hand, its appeal as a venue that can compensate for their social shortcomings can make it addictive. Among introverts, for example, social success on the Internet could lead to an exclusive focus on online life, with no further attempt to improve offline social skills.

The rise of social networks, in which users are typically meant to be identified, has created a challenge for introverts. When social networks began to emerge as a global presence, it was immediately clear that they would become a significant channel of social interaction, where, by definition, anonymity was not possible. This situation was also a challenge for us, researchers, and we wanted to discover how using a social networks affects the use of older online social channels, such as chat forums, where people interacted socially before social networks became established. Research tended to focus on introverts and extroverts, because it was already established that introverts are likely to use anonymous online forums to express their social needs. In a 2005 study I conducted together with Hadar Kaplan and Nira Dorpatcheon, two of my research students, we examined the question of who benefits from the Internet by comparing users and non-users of social networks. (Recall that 2005 was in the earliest days of such networks.) Among each population, we compared introverted and extroverted social network users. The study indicated that extroverts using social networks took more advantage of the Internet's social features (chats, forums, and fantasy worlds) than did introverts. Conversely, among users who did not use social networks but engaged instead in mostly anonymous surfing, the tendency was reversed. That is, in anonymous settings, the introverts made more use of the Internet's social features such as chat forums and fantasy worlds than did extroverts.

The results indicate two different patterns of Internet use. On the one hand, among social network users there was a pattern of preserving one's pre-existing social identity, much like the concept that "the rich get richer." These users, whether introverts or extroverts, in essence reinforced their familiar identities because, as they surfed social networks, they generally encountered friends from their offline lives. Thus the introverts had trouble creating a new persona even outside the social network arena. On the other hand, when we looked at those users who did not use social networks, we saw a different pattern of behavior, more akin to "the poor get richer." These introverts, on entering a new Internet world where they were completely protected, were able to re-assemble themselves, try new social experiences, shake off the chains of their offline identities, and successfully express themselves in the online social arena.

This study taught us about the psychological benefits of the Internet. That is, it has created a complex, multilayered reality where, for both introverts and extroverts, the benefits available are linked to people's online behavioral style. So, it seemed at that stage, that social networks were not benefiting introverts; rather, they created yet another channel through which extroverts could express themselves in addition to offline channels where they already dominated.

In a study I conducted in 2010 with the late Gideon Vinitzky (Amichai-Hamburger & Vinitzky, 2010), a good friend and research colleague, we challenged the supposition that extroverts function well in one environment and introverts in another. We examined whether the personalities of users are linked to their behavior on Facebook. In this study, the users were asked to allow the researchers to enter their Facebook territory in order to see what they were doing and what they weren't, the objective being to capture the most genuine and timely picture of their activity. As we'd expected, the extroverts were more active on Facebook than the introverts. However, one very interesting finding in this study was that introverts invest more time in the construction of their profile than do extroverts. The introverted users supplied a great deal of personal information such as activities they enjoyed, their interests, and favorite music, television programs, books and so on.

It seems that, for introverts, working on their profile is a fairly sheltered activity, with little of the tension associated with real-time interaction. It thus appears that, although social networks do boost extroverts, introverts nonetheless also enjoy certain opportunities for compensating for their social difficulties, specifically by investing in their profiles – which indeed are the identity card that users present to the world.

It is important to stress that, although social networks seem to occupy a more dominant position than anonymous online environments, the latter are still powerful and play a significant role for people online. People who are shy are still more likely to use the anonymous online environments. However, some extroverts also feel better able to express themselves freely on anonymous websites. You may be an extrovert and very active on Facebook, but still desire anonymity before writing a comment on the prime minister's speech, or participating in a discussion group, a fact which you do not wish to share with others. It seems that the need for anonymity has not died and will not do so in the foreseeable future.

The extroversion–introversion personality theory supplies powerful proof that personality is relevant to the Internet. This is the theory that received most attention from researchers, who saw it as particularly relevant to online behavior. Other personality theories were also found to be relevant, however, and we will focus on those next.

WHAT OTHER PERSONALITY THEORIES ARE RELEVANT TO INTERNET USE?

NEED FOR CLOSURE

Try to recall the last occasion on which you had to make a significant decision with your spouse or partner. Did you feel that you needed more information and thus kept delaying the decision, while the other person made their decision much faster? This has to do partly with the personality characteristic called *need for closure*. According to the need for closure theory, people who have a high need for such are motivated to avoid uncertainties. They tend to "freeze" the deliberation process (Kruglanski & Freund, 1983) in order to reach conclusions speedily. They also tend to become fixated on certain concepts and ignore contradicting information. People with a low need for closure are predisposed to "unfreezing" many alternative hypotheses and to test as many implications of their own hypothesis as possible.

PERSONALITY AND NEED FOR CLOSURE

Answer the following questions to ascertain your level of need for closure:

1. When I shop I usually don't follow a definite list.
   Yes/No
2. I often change my plans.
   Yes/No
3. I usually see many different solutions to a given problem.
   Yes/No
4. I don't like living according to a rigid routine.
   Yes/No
5. I like unpredictable situations.
   Yes/No

If you answered all these questions positively you are probably low in need for closure; if you answered negatively, you are probably high in need for closure.

For a more detailed analysis, see Kruglanski, Webster, & Klem's (1993) questionnaire.

In relation to the Internet, need for closure theory is relevant to a question that many web-builders ask themselves: Do people actually like hyperlinks? According to the orthodoxy of web-builders, hyperlinks (text that you can click on to lead you to another web page) are the essence of a good website. It is, however, possible that people who have a high need for closure, namely, a need for a structured and defined process of decision making, will find a plethora of hyperlinks distracting and unnecessary. Conversely, those people with a low need for closure will feel better in an Internet environment surrounded by hyperlinks. If this personality differentiation is confirmed it may explain why some people do not like the net surfing experience, while others do. Amichai-Hamburger and Fine Goldstein (2004) examined this question. The results confirm that, under regular time constraints, people with a low need for closure prefer a website with many hyperlinks, while those with a high need for closure prefer a "flatter" website, that is, with fewer hyperlinks.

NARCISSISM

The Internet is a narcissist's paradise. The term *narcissism*, which means loving yourself too much, derives from Greek mythology. Narcissus, the son of a river god and a nymph named Liriope, was a handsome young man who spurned all the girls who fell in love with him. To punish him for his haughtiness and disregard for the feelings of others, the gods made him fall hopelessly in love with himself. When Narcissus went to drink from a clear pool, he couldn't take his eyes from his own reflection on the glassy surface. Eventually he died there, and the flower we call the narcissus, notable for its beauty, grew where he'd lingered.

In the late nineteenth century, the term narcissism – indicating a feeling of pride that is greater than normal and hurts other people's feelings – began to take on a psychological meaning. In 1914 Freud added his interpretation, claiming that narcissism is a vital natural phase in healthy human development, but so is learning how to feel love for others. The transition from early or "primary" narcissism (love of one's self) to the investment of energy in an external love object, Freud believed, is a crucial step in the individual's healthy development.

PERSONALITY: NARCISSISM

To gain an indication of whether you have narcissistic tendencies, answer the following questions:

1. I like to be the center of attention.
   Yes/No
2. I think I am a special person.
   Yes/No
3. I insist upon getting the respect that is due to me.
   Yes/No
4. Manipulating people is easy.
   Yes/No
5. I am more capable than other people.
   Yes/No
6. I am going to be a great person.
   Yes/No

If you answered all these questions positively, you probably do have narcissistic tendencies. For a better indication of your narcissistic tendencies, complete the questionnaire by Ames Rose & Anderson (2006).

Various Internet platforms, such as blogs, chatrooms, and forums, provide an ideal environment for narcissists to reinforce the sense of their own importance; they can focus on themselves and describe to all who care to listen (or, indeed, who don't) what they've seen, heard, and felt. Social networks, for example, are another place where narcissists can present and "sell" themselves. Narcissists tend to use social networks as a way of cultivating their own standing among others. They take selfies (self-captured photos of themselves), and continuously upload them; they invest a great deal of time in improving their personal profiles; they deliberate at length as they choose pictures, and their posts tend to focus on how "I did..., I do..., I am..." (Wang et al., 2012).

Discourse of this sort provides no real intimacy because the narcissists are completely focused on presenting their own particulars and make no real effort to listen to other people, much less conduct a conversation with depth and meaning. Studies indicate that narcissism is a constantly increasing tendency; more and more people are feeling self-important with increasingly disproportionate egos. According to a comprehensive survey by Konrath O'Brien and Hsing (2011) from the University of Michigan, many people are displaying a steep drop in empathy (being sensitive to, and identifying with, other people's feelings). Some people glumly call today's young people "Generation N," the narcissist generation. That may be a broad generalization, but the trend is an obvious cause for concern.

ATTACHMENT THEORY

Think about your early childhood. Did you have parents who simultaneously gave you a strong sense of being protected and engendered in you the courage to explore the world and its opportunities? John Bowlby, a British psychologist, claimed that people's basic sense of security and their self-esteem are built on the basis of the quality of the social relationships developed with early care-givers. Based on Bowlby's theory, other researchers contributed additional developments that led to the current preferred reliable and valid measure of individual differences known as the Experiences in Close Relationship Scale (ECR; for example, see Brennan, Clark, & Shaver, 1998). This tool was developed for assessing intimacy between partners and categorizes adults on two independent dimensions: (i) anxiety and (ii) avoidance. The anxiety dimension represents the extent to which individuals are concerned that a partner will not be available and responsive during their times of need. The avoidance dimension represents the extent to which individuals lack trust in their partners' goodwill and consequently strive to maintain behavioral independence and emotional distance from them. Individuals who score low on the anxiety and/or avoidant attachment dimensions are generally more secure and have a tendency to utilize constructive and effective strategies for emotional self-regulation. In other words, they have the ability to react using a range of emotions, in a manner that is socially acceptable and allows for spontaneity, as well as being able to delay what would be spontaneous reactions, as needed. On the other hand, individuals who score high on either or both of these dimensions tend to suffer from various forms of insecurity in their relationships; they rely on hyper-activation or de-activation to cope. High avoidance relationship patterns include needing distance from significant others, a tendency to be self-reliant, and fleeing from emotional situations. In contrast, individuals with high anxiety place a great deal of importance on relationships and are strongly motivated to form them. They seek out intimacy and sometimes may put too much pressure on their relationships; these individuals have a high fear of abandonment.

PERSONALITY: ATTACHMENT

Are you the secure type? To gain an indication of how secure you are, answer the following questions:

1. I know that others will be there for me when I need them.
   Yes/No
2. I do not often worry about being abandoned.
   Yes/No
3. I find it easy to get close to others.
   Yes/No
4. I expect the best to happen in a new relationship.
   Yes/No
5. Generally speaking, I feel safe in the world.
   Yes/No

If you answered all these questions positively, you are probably a secure type; if you answered negatively, you are probably an insecure type.

For a fuller picture of your security level, see Brennan, Clark, & Shaver (1998).

In a 2014 study, Yaakobi and Goldenberg found that, in relation to social networks, people with a secure sense of attachment had more social ties and a higher willingness to initiate web-based relationships. They were also more likely to be network leaders. They also found that a decrease in avoidance scores predicted an increased willingness to deliver information to others. This may explain why secure individuals have a higher number of connections. Yaakobi and Goldenberg also found that an increase in anxiety score predicted a decrease in willingness to deliver information to others. These findings suggest that attachment theory can explain the dynamics involved in web-based dissemination of information.

SENSATION-SEEKING

Sensation-seeking is a personality trait defined by the search for new, diverse and intense experiences and feelings, accompanied by a readiness to take risks in their pursuit.

PERSONALITY: SENSATION-SEEKING

Answer the following questions to gain an indication of how sensation-seeking you are:

1. I like wild parties.
   Yes/No
2. I like dangerous situations.
   Yes/No
3. I enjoy extreme sports.
   Yes/No
4. I look for excitement.
   Yes/No
5. I find being in routine environments difficult.
   Yes/No

If you answered all these questions positively, you are probably highly sensation-seeking; if you answered negatively, you probably demonstrate a low level of sensation-seeking. See Zuckerman (1983) for a fuller picture.

The sensation-seeking concept was developed by Marvin Zuckerman of the University of Delaware. Later, Wang et al. (2012) found that people using social networks tend to display a higher level of sensation-seeking behavior. They also found a relationship between gaming addiction and sensation-seeking. The Internet, with all the exciting activities it offers, appears to be very attractive to sensation-seekers; unfortunately, this excitement is sometimes likely to take the form of addiction (Mehroof & Griffiths, 2010).

A FINAL WORD

The experience of introverts on the web is an example of how the Internet can change the lives of individuals and groups. Truly, the Internet makes possible new opportunities and experiences and empowers many types of personality. To understand the psychological factors associated with the Internet, we have turned to a variety of theories to help us understand how certain individuals respond to the online environment. In the case of introverts, for example, we have seen how the Internet presents a double-edged sword: it allows them to compensate for their social difficulties but, as a result, its draw may be so powerful as to very easily become addictive.

Many more personality theories are very likely to be relevant to online behavior, and I believe that with further research this will become apparent. I very much hope that this knowledge will be utilized to enhance the psychological well-being of individuals based on their personalities. However, I am fearful that that same knowledge will be accessed by business interests with the aim of exploiting it in order to better understand how to manipulate people; for example, by promoting an addiction to specific online services, or marketing products based on the knowledge of people's personalities.

REFERENCES

Ames, R. D., Rose, P., & Anderson, P. C. (2006). The NPI-16 as a short measure of narcissism. *Journal of Research in Personality*, 40, 440–450.

Amichai-Hamburger, Y., & Hayat, Z. (2013). Personality and the Internet. In Y. Amichai-Hamburger (Ed.), *The Social Net: Understanding Our Online Behavior* (pp. 1–20). New York: Oxford University Press.

ADAA. (2007) *A Report of the Anxiety Disorders Association of America.* www.adaa.org/sites/default/files/FINALCollegeReport.pdf.

Ames, R. D, Rose, P., & Anderson, P. C. (2006). The NPI-16 as a short measure of narcissism. *Journal of Research in Personality*, 40, 440–450.

Amichai-Hamburger, Y., & Hayat, Z. (2013). Personality and the Internet. In Y. Amichai-Hamburger (Ed.), *The Social Net: Understanding Our Online Behavior* (pp. 1–20). New York: Oxford University Press.

Amichai-Hamburger, Y., & Vinitzky, G. (2010). Social network use and personality. *Computers in Human Behavior, 26*, 1289–1295.

Amichai-Hamburger, Y., Kaplan, H., & Dorpatcheon, N. (2008). Click to the past: The impact of extroversion by users of nostalgic websites on the use of Internet social services. *Computers in Human Behavior, 24*, 1907–1912.

Amichai-Hamburger, Y., Wainapel, G., & Fox, S. (2002). "On the internet no one knows I'm an introvert": Extroversion, neuroticism, and internet interaction. *CyberPsychology and Behavior, 2*, 125–128.

Amichai-Hamburger, Y., Fine, A., & Goldstein, A. (2004). The impact of Internet interactivity and need for closure on consumer preference. *Computers in Human Behavior, 20*, 103–117.

Amichai-Hamburger, Y., Lamdan, N., Madiel, R., & Hayat, T. (2008). Personality characteristics of Wikipedia members. *Cyberpsychology and Behavior, 11*, 679–681.

Anolli, L., Villani, D., & Riva, G. (2005). Personality of people using chat: An on-line research. *CyberPsychology and Behavior, 8*, 89–94.

Bargh, J. A., McKenna, K. Y. A., & Fitzsimons, G. (2002). Can you see the real me? Activation and expression of the "true self" on the Internet. *Journal of Social Issues, 58*, 33–48.

Dunn, R. A., & Guadagno, R. E. (2012). My avatar and me? Gender and personality predictors of avatar–self discrepancy. *Computers in Human Behavior, 28*, 97–106.

Eysenck, H. J., & Eysenck, S. E. G. (1975). *Manual: Eysenck Personality Inventory.* San Diego, CA: Educational and Industrial Testing Service.

Guadagno, R. E., Okdie, B. M., & Eno, C. A. (2008). Who blogs? Personality predictors of blogging. *Computers in Human Behavior, 24*, 1993–2004.

Hamburger, Y. A., & Ben-Artzi, E. (2000). The relationship between extraversion and neuroticism and the different uses of the Internet. *Computers in Human Behavior, 16*, 441–449.

Konrath, S., O'Brien, E., & Hsing, C. (2011). Changes in dispositional empathy in American college students over time: A meta-analysis. *Personality and Social Psychology Review, 15*, 180–198.

Kraut, R., Kiesler, S., Boneva, B., Cummings, J., Helgeson, V., & Crawford, A. (2002). Internet paradox revisited. *Journal of Social Issues, 58*, 49–57.

Kruglanski, A. W., & Freund, T. (1983). The freezing and unfreezing of lay inferences: Effects of impressional primacy, ethnic stereotyping and numerical anchoring. *Journal of Experimental Social Psychology, 19*, 448–468.

Kruglanski, A. W., & Webster, D. M. (1996). Motivated closing of the mind: "Seizing" and "freezing." *Psychological Review, 103*, 263–283.

Kruglanski, A. W., Webster, D. M., & Klem, A. (1993). Motivated resistance and openness to persuasion in the presence or absence of prior information. *Journal of Personality & Social Psychology*, 65, 861–876.

Manhal-Baugus, M. (2001). E-therapy: Practical, ethical, and legal issues. *Cyberpsychology & Behavior*, 4, 551–563.

Mehroof, M., & Griffiths M. D. (2010). Online gaming addiction: The role of sensation seeking, self-control, neuroticism, aggression, state anxiety, and trait anxiety. *CyberPsychology, Behavior, and Social Networking*, 13, 313–316.

Pervin, L. A. (1993). *Personality: Theory and Research*. New York: Wiley.

Posner, K., Melvin, G. A., Stanley, B., Oquendo, M. A., & Gould, M. (2007). Factors in the assessment of suicidality in youth. *CNS Spectrums*, 12, 156–162.

Stanley, B., Brown, G., Brent, D. A., Wells, K., Poling, K., Curry, J., et al. (2008). Cognitive behavior therapy for suicide prevention (CBT-SP): Treatment model, feasibility and acceptability. *Journal of the American Academy of Child and Adolescent Psychiatry*, 48, 1005–1013.

Sue, S. (2006). Cultural competency: From philosophy to research and practice. *Journal of Community Psychology*, 34, 237–245.

Wang, J. L., Jackson, L. A., Zhang, D. J., & Su, Z. Q. (2012). The relationships among the Big Five personality factors, self-esteem, narcissism, and sensation-seeking to Chinese university students' uses of social networking sites (SNSs). *Computers in Human Behavior*, 28, 2313–2319.

Witte, T. K., Gould, M. S., Munfakh, J. L. H., Kleinman, M., Joiner, T. E., & Kalafat, J. (2010). Assessing suicide risk among callers to crisis hotlines: A confirmatory factor analysis. *Journal of Clinical Psychology*, 66, 941–964.

Wright, J., Stepney, S., Clark, J. A., & Jacob, J. L. (2005). *Formalizing anonymity: A review*. University of York Technical Report YCS 389.

Yaakobi, E., & Goldenberg, J. (2014). Social relationships and information dissemination in virtual social network systems: An attachment theory perspective. *Computers in Human Behavior*, 38, 127–135.

Yang, H.-L., & Lai, C.-Y. (2010). Motivations of Wikipedia content contributors. *Computers in Human Behavior*, 26, 1377–1383.

Zuckerman, M. (1983). *Biological Bases of Sensation Seeking, Impulsivity and Anxiety*. Hillsdale, NJ: Erlbaum.

3

IS TRUE LOVE OBTAINABLE VIA THE INTERNET?

On the web, I'm who I really am.
No games, no faking, no masks.
The love I have on the web...
that's real love.

– anonymous web surfer

The Beatles went straight to the point when they stated, or rather sang, *All you need is love*. Truly, love is essential to our happiness and well-being as human beings. In this chapter we will be delving into many different aspects of love and romance to see how they play out in the online world. We will ask: What is love? Can you find real love online? How can we differentiate between intimacy and public relations? Why do we trust people online so speedily? What is the attraction of total online love? When is it legitimate to manipulate our personal details in the online environment? What roles do concealment and openness play in online romance? We will also be taking a look at the phenomenon of falling in love with a celebrity and examining how real such love is.

WHAT IS THE IMPORTANCE OF LOVE IN OUR LIFE?

The warmth of love is strongly related to our happiness in life. The late, world-renowned psychologist Michael Argyle, my doctoral advisor at Oxford, was the pioneer who translated happiness from something expressed in dance, song, and prose as an abstraction into something that can be measured and researched (Argyle, 1987). In a series of studies, Argyle (1987) found that a mutual romantic relationship is the most significant source of satisfaction with life. Unfortunately, the flip-side of this is that the inability to form significant romantic relationships may lead to a lower level of happiness and a general dissatisfaction with life.

Through later studies, evidence of the positive impact of love has extended to many aspects of our life. For example, Younger et al.'s (2010) study at Stanford University found that people in the passionate stage of love (i.e., within the first nine months of their relationship) who were shown photographs of their romantic partner exhibited increased activation in those parts of the brain associated with pain blocking, and demonstrated reduction in the experience of pain.

MINI-BIOGRAPHY: MICHAEL ARGYLE, PIONEER OF SOCIAL SKILLS TRAINING

Michael Argyle (1925–2002) was one of the best-known social psychologists of the twentieth century. He spent most of his career in the Department of Psychology at the University of Oxford. Argyle was a pioneer in many research fields. He applied experimental methods to fields that had never been researched empirically, and, by doing so, extended the borders of experimental social psychology. Argyle was one of the first to bring interpersonal relationships to the lab, with the most creative research methods. His groundbreaking research in the area of happiness and well-being helped identify the main factors in life that contribute to psychological well-being. He applied his research findings to his own social life; in fact, his social research group parties were famous. Naturally gregarious, he attracted many distinguished minds from the fields of psychology and sociology, many of whom came from all over the world to visit him in Oxford. His perception of a psychologist was someone who is very involved in the world: not merely an observer, but a participant. I still remember him telling me that "more important than the lecture, is the visit to the pub afterwards." As a very optimistic person and a change agent, he transmitted this spirit to the people around him.

WHAT IS LOVE?

Let's start with the basics – how can we define love? Most people recognize love when they feel it, but no fully agreed upon psychological explanation of what love is exists. Rather than using a single concrete definition, we'll focus on three different approaches to understanding what love is. Each looks at love from a different angle, and, combined, these three approaches may offer a more complete picture of love. In the first approach, love is an interpretation of physiological arousal; in the second, love is commerce – a type of trade transaction; and, in the third, it is an emotional phenomenon.

PHYSIOLOGY

The first approach centers on physiology. According to this approach, the idea of love can be separated into two parts: the physical arousal that a person feels for no apparent reason, and the interpretation of that arousal as love. In other words, if we experience intense physical arousal in the presence of a particular person and cannot explain this sensation, we will often see this as evidence that we've fallen in love (Cotton, 1981).

A study carried out in Vancouver, Canada, by Dutton and Aron (1974), examined the effect of physical excitement on attraction between the sexes. Men were approached after crossing a bridge. One group crossed a wire-cable bridge swaying over a deep chasm (the Capilano suspension bridge, if you want to repeat the experiment). The other group crossed a stable bridge a mere ten feet from the ground. The researchers expected that participants would experience a much higher level of excitement after crossing the former bridge.

To test this hypothesis, immediately after crossing their particular bridge the participants were asked by a researcher to complete a questionnaire about a research project. Some participants were approached by a male researcher, and others by a female researcher. Each participant received the researcher's phone number, ostensibly in case they wanted more information about the project and its results.

Next, the participants were given a projective test; that is, they were shown ambiguous pictures on cards and asked to provide the story behind each one. Those men who had crossed the frightening bridge provided female researchers with much more sexual interpretations of the pictures. Moreover, men who had crossed the frightening bridge also phoned the female researchers much more often than they did the male researchers. According to the physiological theory, the strong excitement (a narrow, shaky bridge), together with an appropriate hint (the female researcher with the questionnaire), caused the male participants to attribute the pulsation of their blood and their general excitement to a romantic attraction to the researcher, rather than to fear.

COMMERCE

A more cynical approach to love involves the concept of social commerce (Sabatell, 1988). This approach considers every social relationship as part of a system of trading, with give and take, expenses and income. In this context, love is the result of two people finding compatibility in terms of social standing, attractiveness, and abilities.

Social standing comes into play in terms of how society ranks the social class that each person is seen as belonging to. *Attractiveness* is defined according to culture, and in the West involves many criteria not merely physical appearance. *Abilities* can reflect both inborn potential (such as IQ) and acquired skills (such as a promising profession). According to the theory of social tradeoffs, people will try to find mates who are the closest match according to those three systems of ranking. The ideal couple would rank similarly in all three ways – equally high or equally low.

However, the theory of social tradeoffs also allows for cross-balancing between criteria. Thus, for example, an ugly billionaire would rank low in attractiveness, but high in social standing and could choose an attractive woman for himself – assuming, of course, that the woman does not already have all the wealth she desires.

The more pleased the individuals are with the balance of tradeoffs, the longer, stronger, and more satisfactory the relationship is likely to be for them. In this way, love is a deal akin to a commercial transaction, and everyone likes to see a good return on their investment.

Such a model for understanding love also helps contextualize certain taboos. For example, if a man pursues a woman who ranks higher socially than he does, he risks various forms of punishment that may include mockery, social sanctions, and isolation, depending on the social milieu.

EMOTIONS

The emotion-centered approach (Rubin, 1973) views love as a combined answer to several different human needs. The human need for company and physical contact has to do with *attachment*. The feeling of genuine concern has to do with *caring*. And the desire to share and to involve the other person in our own individual life, in a way beyond what we would offer to anyone else, has to do with *intimacy*. When attachment, caring, and intimacy combine intensely, the combination is love.

CAN YOU FIND REAL LOVE ONLINE?

In the first days of the Internet, love was assumed to be irrelevant to the online world. In those days, messages between people were purely textual; the number of Internet users was small, and no areas were set aside for matchmaking. The prevailing view was that such a significant intimate process as falling in love had no chance of success in such a limited context of communication. However, as the Internet developed, it became easier and more natural to meet new people and create romantic connections. This phenomenon is reflected in what we have termed the Magnificent Seven – the special combination of qualities unique to the web. (See Chapter 1 for a full discussion of the qualities that make web-surfing unique.) The feeling of anonymity on the web contributes to the likelihood that we will express ourselves more freely online than offline, and perhaps in this way be more likely to form significant connections faster. Since the net allows people to craft and recraft their message, according to their own schedule, to their satisfaction, people feel a high degree of control over communication; for many, this is a way of bypassing the obstacles and challenges of everyday life that stand in the way of acquiring a mate. For people with low self-esteem, or with problems relating to body image, the control over their level of physical exposure is a blessing, allowing them to connect with people on the basis of personality rather than external appearance. This is relevant for someone who is not satisfied with their looks and, conversely, also for a physically attractive person who wants to know that people like them for their personality. The ease of locating similar people on the web can be very helpful in finding a mate with compatible interests, especially when such people are not easy to find. The web's accessibility and availability at all times and places can raise the level of immediacy and satisfaction in the Internet romance. The net's egalitarianism can prompt the courage to dare pursue a romance even if it may break the traditional rules of suitability. And finally, the fun of web surfing can add value to an online romance and often turn it into a mixture of game and reality.

Indeed, when we look at today's Internet we see that it has changed from a clubhouse for techie nerds into a public space, and as of now is the most significant public space for the pursuit of love. The web includes many focused areas for finding love, from a whole range of matchmaking sites to chatrooms, acquaintanceship forums, fantasy games, and social networks, all frequented by many people in search of love. Some search with more success, some with less, but for many the Internet is an excellent place to initiate romance.

There are those who vehemently disagree; they argue that online love, if it exists at all, is a poor, partial, unfulfilling substitute for real love.

I believe that the web is a very significant place in which to find love and below I will go further to suggest that this is the case even when it is based on text interactions alone. This contradicts one of the primary criticisms of the notion of online love, which claims that text alone cannot convey love's power. Such a claim is actually quite strange, when we consider the power of writing about love in poetry and prose, from the romances of Shakespeare to the sonnets of Elizabeth Barrett Browning (an English poet of the Victorian era). Moreover, love letters have always gripped the imagination. Today we are privy to the love letters of many famous historical figures, for example Napoleon's letters to Joséphine de Beauharnais, or Churchill's to Clementine Hozier.

All those examples, and many more, show that words can express love forcefully. The Internet, meanwhile, has come to provide many tools besides text, including video chats in which the couple can speak to and see one another. Let's see how the theories of love we mentioned before relate to the Internet:

By focusing on the interpretation of physical excitement, the physiology approach asserts that essentially love is just the explanation we provide for an otherwise unexplained sense of physical arousal. In other words, love occurs when the brain decides that it must be occurring.

Some people may believe that such a theory is not relevant to the Internet, since in many cases, initially, it's impossible to know what the other person really looks like, and they may be much less attractive than you imagine. However, the strongest rebuttal to that claim is that the Internet didn't invent subjective perception, imagination, or fantasy. Beauty has always existed in the eyes of the beholder. When we're in love, our minds create an idealized image that others may not agree with. They may find it surprising, or even ridiculous. Nobody can see the beloved in the same way the lover does. Others might see little intelligence or beauty where the lover perceives perfection. In fact, the role of fantasy in a romantic relationship is often significant, and on the Internet it can frequently reach a peak.

Our brains are constantly attempting to understand and profile those with whom we come into contact, even when a great deal of information is missing, especially when an exchange of text messages is the only interaction. Our behavior on the Internet is no exception. In some cases we depend completely on the other party for providing what we consider basic information, for example how they look. This is when we bring into play our wishful thinking and our need to fulfill our fantasies. Most likely, we will buy into the information they give us about how they look, their education, their financial situation, and any other data they offer to describe themselves. When they provide partial information, we tend to close the gaps with very positive information that glorifies them. In some cases the target of love even "cooperates" actively with us by engaging in a kind of "reading between the lines," that is, sensing what we wish for and then providing it. This is especially the case when the target of love gains information regarding how they *should* be and is willing to play into the fantasy. When it comes to fantasy, it is amazing just how quickly and easily we trust the other person.

CHATROOM: ONE MAN'S ACCOUNT OF INTERNET DATING

Consider this story of a married man's online dalliance, and what he knows about his online paramour.

> *I'm on chat with a girl, the most amazing person I've ever met. This girl is tall, with short brown hair – just what I like. She has the biggest blue eyes you'll see in your life. I haven't seen a picture yet, but she described herself thoroughly. And what's more, she'll have her doctorate soon. Anyway, we have the most amazing chats. She's charismatic, sexy, a-may-zing.... My wife is reduced to a pale reality. (Ben Ze'ev, 2009, p. 330)*

Yes, this man has found the love of his life. He concedes that he has no picture yet, but he doesn't doubt that she gave a true description. Upon discovering that in every detail she precisely matches the perfect woman he's sought all his life, he still doesn't feel a trace of suspicion. And there's a bonus: this beauty is about to receive a doctorate. Beauty and brains together. If that's not perfection, what is? We want to think we are worthy of our fantasy, so we start to believe in it: we build trust as we dive deeper and deeper into our fantasy. This can very easily lead to a situation in which people prefer to interact with their online romantic partner, and come to see their offline partner as boring and unappealing. At the end of the day, it is all in our head.

Meanwhile, the emotion-centered approach to understanding love sees it as a combination of attachment, caring, and intimacy. The Internet can easily convey caring and intimacy – concern for the other and the sharing of life's personal details, respectively. However, attachment is a bit more complicated as it involves the desire to be together, to have physical contact with the lover. On the one hand, lovers can sometimes be more available to one another online than off because they can be together using smartphones, which can create the feeling of a real presence although they are not physically together. On the other hand, online love is missing the physical dimension (at least initially). In many cases the Internet provides the initial acquaintanceship, in a safe environment and accompanied by a strong sense of personal control. When people feel comfortable in that type of relationship, they will organize a face-to-face meeting. In some cases, though, the lovers prefer the online world and do not cross into the physical realm, and nonetheless still consider themselves in a love relationship to all intents and purposes.

Another approach to love, described above, considered it in terms of a transaction – What do I give and what do I get? – akin to a commercial arrangement, involving a significant attempt to create the best match. We all have a social credit card that determines what we can "buy" in the relationship, and who is likely to try and "buy" us. On the Internet the transactions are quite clear and simple. Consider matchmaking websites, for example. Various websites address specific target audiences: they state in advance who is suitable for membership, and also try to make sure that no one unsuitable is allowed access. The working assumption on the matchmaking sites is that each of us carries a sort of social "credit rating" that defines our status as compared to others. Such a site might filter out everyone but postgraduates, or those declaring a particular financial status. In order to sign up to a specific matchmaking site, you must be found suitable on the basis of what you bring to the match. When you have gained access, you must catalog yourself according to various criteria. Then the site will help you find someone who matches your social credit rating. Some matchmaking websites are generic; members need only pay the subscription fee. However, these sites also help members categorize themselves to help ensure the best match according to each person's social credit card.

In recent years, just as everything else has migrated to Facebook, groups of singles have evolved there, too. A friend of a single person, for example, may post a search for a match, and the Facebook page can then serve as a filter for assessing candidates according to the social credit rating that's desired.

In this context, it should be remembered that some people think of everything in life in terms of personal profit and loss. They're always on the lookout for a better deal, whether in real estate or romance. Such people sometimes leave a romantic relationship not because they're unhappy, but because they've found a better opportunity. The potential they imagine provides sufficient reason to abandon a successful relationship (Rusbult, 1980). Such people will see the Internet as an endless market, and they therefore are likely to leap from one "romantic" partner to another in a perpetual effort to increase their profits.

Another important point regarding achieving the best match with your social credit card is the credibility of information. On Facebook you depend totally on how the person describes him- or herself, which of course may not be fully accurate. Also, in the case of matchmaking websites, most are not making sufficient effort to verify the information given to love-seekers, even on sites that charge a membership fee. At this point, it is worth looking more carefully at how the element of fantasy can affect the way we understand intimacy.

CHATROOM: CHARLES, THE ONLINE SOCIAL CLIMBER

Charles is happily married to Beth. They have two sweet daughters, Annabelle, 6, and Victoria, 3. They live in an amazing cottage in Devon, England. Everything looks great for them but behind the happy ideal image lies a somewhat less ideal reality. Charles is happy in his relationship with Beth; growing up together in the village, they always knew that they were born for each other. However, Charles is a woman hunter, and has always been so. He is constantly looking at other women – especially those whose social status he perceives to be higher than his own – and imagining what it would be like to be in a relationship with them.

Offline, Charles is too reserved and inhibited to translate his ambitions into real action; however, when he discovered the Internet, he realized that he had found the perfect playground for his social-climbing ambitions. He initiates anonymous chats with an endless stream of women but, every so often, finds a romantic partner who fits his social-climbing dream, and then focuses on her exclusively. However, Charles has noticed that, after a few weeks of speaking only with one woman, he begins to look for someone even better. He feels that he needs someone more exciting, more brilliant, from a more elite background. Recently he met Liz, an upper-class, well-educated, bountiful partner. As he became more acquainted with Liz, he began to feel more impatient with his wife. Her social credit card seemed very meager in comparison to that of his new woman. His wife's conversations appeared so boring, focusing on domestic issues or her friends. This was even more the case when he compared them with chats with Liz, the student of international relations in her late twenties.

INTIMACY: WHAT HAPPENS WHEN WE FALL IN LOVE WITH A FANTASY?

Intimacy is a very sensitive and illusive component in relationships (Reis & Shaver, 1988). A relationship involves a long journey of mutual emotional discovery. A sense of intimacy results from feeling closeness and warmth. When we feel intimate, we can remove our defenses and share our inner world. We feel that we can stop acting and be who we really are; we can express our emotions and allow our partner to do the same. Intimacy is lifelong journey. To make it happen, many factors need to come into play. Among the most important are (1) positive framing for the partner and the relationship, and (2) the creation of opportunities for intimacy whereby you can focus on each other and your relationship. Achieving a sense of intimacy is difficult. It has become even harder as it conflicts with the contemporary view that time equals money. This drive for efficiency has resulted in the need for multitasking. Spending time with loved ones without being interrupted is thus becoming increasingly impossible. A modern hug is often portrayed – humorously – as two people clasping each other while simultaneously checking their smartphones. This caricature reflects the decline in people's level of intimacy. Let's ask a direct question: What generally happens when you are with your partner and your phone alerts you to an email or Facebook post? Do you briefly scan it? Most people admit that they would. They'll justify doing so by stating that they're waiting for an important message, are expected to be available to their boss, and so on. In a piece of research that I conducted recently with my research assistant, Shir Etgar, we found that such behavior is harmful to the level of intimacy within a relationship. Also, each partner justifies their own action in checking their phone as necessary but views the behavior of the other as damaging to their time together. Psychologists call such justification *attribution bias*; each person is able to justify their own actions, but when their partner behaves in the same way, it is perceived as being very bad for intimacy and harmful to the relationship (Amichai-Hamburger & Etgar, 2016).

HOW DO INDIVIDUAL DIFFERENCES AFFECT ONLINE LOVE?

For many people, being able to start a romantic interaction with only a limited degree of physical exposure and control over the communication provides a means to compensate for their physical disadvantages. For example, people with hearing problems may be able to pass the first stage of a romantic encounter without dealing with the unfair stereotypes people ascribe to deaf people. The same can be true for people with disabilities or physical characteristics as a result of which they receive unfair, biased treatment. It can also give a headstart to people with social inhibitions, such as very shy introverts who find the early stages in romantic encounters to be especially challenging. The feeling of safety that they experience online makes it much easier for such individuals to express themselves. When they feel more secure in the interaction, they are more likely to build up courage and confidence, which may slowly and gradually lead to them initiating a face-to-face meeting.

CHATROOM: CAN SHY PEOPLE MEET?

A good friend of ours, Sheila, studied in a university in Israel. She was a very shy person and had very limited interaction with men her own age. As part of her degree course, she participated in an online project with a university in the United States. She found herself working on a subtask with student called Jacob who was studying at the American university. Gradually, she began to feel attracted to him and because she was in her own environment and able to shape her online messages when and how she wished, she felt protected and comfortable enough to express herself. The work relationship developed slowly and gradually into an online romance. Eventually he announced that he was coming to Israel to visit her. At that point their relationship became a face-to-face romance and they were soon married. Time has passed, and now they live in Israel and have a happy and healthy family. When I spoke to them about how their relationship developed, Jacob reported that he too is very shy and found that the Internet allowed him to express himself.

WHY DO WE TRUST PEOPLE ONLINE SO SPEEDILY?

Trust and intimacy go hand-in-hand. The safer people feel, the more they open up to others in the spirit of trust (Rempel, Holmes, &

Zanna, 1985). We generally don't reveal intimate details about ourselves to people we're not sure we can trust, for the simple reason that trusting the wrong person can have catastrophic results. Consider, for example, the case of a man who falls in love with a nice-looking woman and quickly concludes that she's his one and only. He immediately trusts her and tells her about the breakdown he suffered after his mother died. Less than a week later, he finds to his astonishment that she has told his traumatic secret to several people. How would you feel in his position? Possibly not only miserable and betrayed, but also foolish for misplacing your trust in that person. The price is great and essentially irreparable – the loss of your privacy.

When the Internet was taking its first steps, there was almost no discussion about online intimacy. Many net-based interactions were between strangers – it seemed inconceivable that we would tell highly personal details to virtual strangers.

And yet, it has gradually become apparent that the transition to intimacy often happens faster online than offline. Again this is prompted, particularly in the early stages, by the feeling of safety resulting from the limited physical exposure and the anonymity and control over interactions that the Internet offers. Among the many paradoxes associated with the Internet, that related to intimacy is perhaps the most beguiling. You establish a relationship with someone you know nothing about; you become better acquainted and turn the relationship into something more personal. But despite the intimacy, you can end the relationship at any time, with no effort. And you feel all the more in control because a click of your mouse can return the other person to the depths of cyberspace forever. One might anticipate that this ease of dismissal may make online relationships slow or impossible to progress. However, the reverse appears to be true. Knowing you have the option to cut the other person off at any time, you ask yourself, "What's the worst that could happen?" and quickly start feeling confident enough to express yourself freely. The other party follows suit, slowly becoming more open, and the relationship is on its way to being strengthened by mutual intimacy. For many people, this leads to the feeling of having found their true love online. They describe their online dialog as the most open, fulfilling, and exciting relationship they've ever had. They may speak in terms of "seeing into the heart," meaning that online love has enabled them to truly perceive the other in a real and intimate way (Ben-Ze'ev, 2009).

Although many online relationships turn into offline romances, many people do not want to move their relationship into the offline environment, inviting the question, what exactly do they get from online love?

WHAT IS THE ATTRACTION OF ONLINE LOVE?

Love follows predictable phases. The first phase is courtship: generally involving a sense of attraction to someone and the excitement of getting to know them and finding things in common. The couple may offer the moon to one another, or promise not to become like their parents. They may shower each other with gifts, and enjoy restaurants and entertainment. Importantly, they are both totally invested in the relationship. Sometimes as the relationship stabilizes a sense of routine creeps in, with all its accompanying drabness, commitments, and mundane obligations to each other. These may not be obligations that they're eager to meet, but they each insist they're part of the relationship. That's the thorn within the rose. The thorn can lurk in annoying little details such as running the dishwasher, carrying the trash out, walking the dog, cleaning the living room, recycling the beer bottles, or visiting the in-laws. In most relationships, the rose outweighs the thorns, so that the relationship can gather strength and endure.

On the other hand, online love, as long as it remains online, can promise a rose without a thorn, at least as long as the relationship remains solely online. The online lover can be reachable everywhere, anytime, so that the couple feel constantly together. That feeling can be palpable, and persist even when the beloved doesn't immediately answer a message. The fact that the couple are always available to one another is enough to provide the impression of togetherness. Add to all that the fact that the online lover is flawless both in beauty and character – a result, as discussed previously, of our own tendency toward fantasy – and love has achieved perfection. No one will tell someone else when to wash the dishes or clean the car. No bothersome or annoying elements will creep into the relationship. Online communication is pure lollipops and roses: the ultimate fantasy come true.

The online-to-offline transition of a romance may shatter the idealization that had previously been attached to the relationship. In fact, the most appealing element of the relationship may be revealed as its all-rose-and-no-thorns character. It benefited from all the positives, without the routine that is ultimately associated with long-term relationships. Now the offline setting suddenly brings out the thorns: things come along that need to be attended to even though they're not so romantic. The magic of the supposedly perfect relationship falls away, and, in some cases, the partners go back to surfing the net in search of their next fantasy.

WHAT ARE THE BOUNDARIES OF ONLINE INFIDELITY?

Some people develop an online relationship alongside their offline romantic commitment. This intense relationship may well have started in a small, noncommittal way, during a short chat, but over time may become addictive. In the obsessive phase, someone may feel the need to message the other person while driving, even with their partner or spouse beside them; or spend the night with them virtually while their actual romantic partner lies on the other side of the bed. The fast pace of the Internet allows the alternative relationship to mushroom from something trivial to the point that the virtual mate casts the real partner in the shade. Hiding such a relationship for long is very difficult, as the perpetrator grows increasingly obsessed with the online love interest.

Here, it is worth considering the boundaries of infidelity. Does an online relationship that's never been physically consummated, and isn't intended to be consummated, count as cheating? Some say no. How could it be, they protest, if no physical contact has ever occurred? What makes it any different from simple daydreaming? But still, most people consider an online affair to be cheating in every way. The investment of time is understood as occurring at the expense of the offline flesh-and-blood partner, and thus is critically harmful to mutual trust.

A romantic mate offline may be chubby rather than thin. Or fifty-five years old rather than twenty. Or the opposite sex rather than the same sex. But the urgings of our heart, our conscious and unconscious desires, draw us into a sometimes addictive world of fantasy. It seems that, in most cases, the flesh-and-blood mate considers such virtual dalliances a threat to real-life togetherness. A mate may respond in exactly the same way to online and physical infidelities; that is, with silent avoidance of the matter, weeping, shouting, break-ups, and even violence.

CHATROOM: THE STORY OF ASHLEY MADISON

The Ashley Madison Agency was founded in 2002 by Darren Morgenstern. It was aimed at married people who wanted to have extra-marital romantic excitement, with an emphasis on discretion. It was proud to be the largest social network of this kind, famous for its slogan: "Life is short. Have an affair." The name of its website was created from two popular female names: "Ashley" and "Madison." In July 2015, hackers broke into the website and stole all the private data from the site: names, addresses, credit card details of patrons, and even the interaction data. The hackers demanded that the website close its activity. After a short while some of the users' names were released to the public and simultaneously public scandals broke, as it was revealed that some major public figures were among the clients of the website.

The "funny" part of the Ashley Madison saga is that many of the female profiles listed on the website were actually made by the male workers of the agency so as to create the impression of a larger presence of female clientele, when in reality females were actually somewhat of a rarity on the site. The story is told that in one case a male worker created a few hundred female profiles. We can see from this amazing story how powerful fantasy is. The male customers of the agency who wanted to fulfill their fantasies came to trust these fake identities. There is a kind of lunacy to the fact that while many men believed that they were interacting with a beautiful girl, they were actually connecting with a male worker from the agency, who in many cases ran several of those fake fantasies, maybe even simultaneously. (Victor, 2015)

WHEN IS IT PERMISSIBLE TO STRETCH OUR PERSONAL DETAILS?

A study conducted by Inbal Moshe of Ben Gurion University of the Negev (2008), which I supervised, examined how people choose their avatar for use in a virtual environment. This study was actually even more specialized because the virtual environment in question also served as a matchmaking arena for avatars, with the knowledge, and indeed intention, that the relationship, once formed, would at some point move offline. Moshe discovered that the people who created avatars adjusted their approach based on what they thought the likelihood would be of actually meeting their significant other via this approach. As the likelihood of such an encounter diminished, the avatar chosen became further and further removed from their actual offline persona. In other words, a tall, thin man with dark hair and glasses, who strongly believes that he is going to meet his soul mate via a particular forum and will soon encounter her face to face, will likely create an avatar who somewhat resembles him. If, however, the opposite is true, and he believes his chance of meeting someone is low, he may be more inclined to produce a muscular blond avatar with perfect eyesight.

Similar results were found on matchmaking websites, where a strong tension exists between the desire to present the perfect self and the desire to present an authentic image. It seems clear that, when people expect to meet the other person, they will pay more heed to the demands of accuracy than perfection (Ellison Heino & Gibbs, 2006).

We also have to bear in mind that what is acceptable in one online environment will not be acceptable in another. For example, a fantasy game is by definition a game. So, it's generally expected that the players will put a twist on reality. The problem begins when people sell a fantasy to others in an environment where such behavior is not acceptable, that is to say, mutually agreed upon. Unfortunately, some people even extend the fantasy past the limits of the law.

TYRONE: AN IMPERCEPTIBLE LOVER

One astonishing true story of online life concerns a charismatic fellow called Tyrone, who induced many female surfers to fall in love with him. He was quick to promise them the moon and stars, and even committed himself to marriage. He received expensive gifts from them, and every so often would request sums of money, "just until the check I'm owed arrives," he claimed. One of the women, who continually sent gifts to her online lover, eventually became suspicious, because although he did send a photograph, he wasn't very eager to meet in person. After some

> sophisticated snooping, she discovered that Tyrone was no attractive man, but actually a creative woman who had found an original way of making some money by selling a fantasy to other women. Tyrone's cover was blown, and the story ends with the scammer being committed to a mental hospital after breaking down under the pressures that descended upon her. It seems, then, that when it's not a fantasy game, people expect you to be honest. (Goldman, 2003)

HOW CAN WE DISTINGUISH BETWEEN REAL INTIMACY AND PUBLIC RELATIONS?

Even when our relationships exist offline, they often have an intense and consequential presence on the Internet, especially on social networks that generate an enormous amount of personal exposure. Facebook is the arena in which you construct the image you wish to display to the world and seek positive reinforcement in the form of "Likes," that is, indicators of approval. Facebook reflects your status as a romantic partner immediately and uncompromisingly. As soon as you're in a relationship, you must immediately change your status to say so, lest you be mistaken for someone who's "looking." You must promptly upload personal pictures, sometimes painfully cheesy ones, of yourself with your new love. And, of course, you mustn't forget to immediately remove images of previous partners.

The next stage is to market your togetherness. Every event you've attended together, every activity, needs to be reported on in the form of text, photos, and videos. Basically, you're committed to constantly marketing yourself as half of a couple.

This invites the question: On what is this relationship actually focused – each other, or a dialogue with the rest of the world? That is, what is intimacy and what is public relations? What happens on social networks can detract from the stability of a relationship, because publicizing everything about themselves may corrode the intimacy between a couple. Their experiences as a couple may become shallow and thus fail to offer the full emotional reward that real intimacy provides.

DO MORE ROMANTIC OPTIONS LEAD TO BETTER DECISIONS?

On the Internet there are many matchmaking websites. Thousands of people are presenting themselves in attractive profiles and attempting to find the right one. Matchmaking websites also use search engines that help you to filter out bad matches. It seems reasonable to assume that more search options would lead to better results; however, the opposite is true. Surprisingly, research demonstrates that more search options actually lead to poorer results in finding the right person. It appears that a glut of search options overloads our cognitive resources and leads us to invest a lot of time on less compatible options and, in many cases, our search for love thus becomes inefficient (Wu & Chiou 2009).

A later study compared what are known as "maximizers" and "satisfiers." The former refers to the kind of person who examines all the options in their search for maximum satisfaction, the type who would typically state, "When I'm in the car listening to the radio, I often check other stations to see if something better is playing even if I'm relatively satisfied with what I'm listening to." This behavior demonstrates a maximizing tendency. People with low maximizing tendencies are known as "satisfiers." The research study in question compared the choice-making strategies of the two groups, focusing on excessive searching, quality of final decisions, and selectivity. Results indicated that the participants with high maximizing tendencies (i.e., maximizers) demonstrated more pronounced searching than did those with low maximizing tendencies (i.e., satisfiers). When we look in terms of selectivity and final choices, the negative effect of excessive searching on decision making was found to be more prominent for maximizers than for satisfiers. These findings reveal that excessive access to options doesn't always lead to better choices or more satisfaction (Yang & Chiou, 2010).

Just before getting to the last word on this chapter I would like to touch upon one interesting relationship that is part of online love, especially for young people: "relationships" with celebrities.

FALLING IN LOVE WITH A CELEBRITY: HOW REAL IS IT?

Celebrities share their lives with their public, via blogs, Instagram, Twitter, YouTube, Facebook, and many other online channels. This situation creates feelings of intimacy between the individual fan and their celebrity of choice. As a fan, you have direct access to the celebrity, cultivating the sense that you really know them, that they really know you, and that their messages are phrased especially for you. However, this is an illusion. It is an asymmetrical intimacy because the celebrity doesn't really know anything about you, and they aren't actually interested in your life. There is no real intimacy, only the illusion of it. Having asymmetrical relationships with celebrities is not a new phenomenon. In the 1950s it was called para-social interaction, and referred to the television; today, following the advent of the Internet, it exists in a much stronger iteration. This is partly due to the large variety of channels that celebrities can use to report to us about almost everything they are doing: from eating their breakfast to buying a new car, enjoying dinner dates to getting a new haircut – and all in real time. Also celebrities are likely, at least on occasion, to interact with one individual follower, creating the possibility that tomorrow it could be you who receives a direct Tweet, for example; often, this strengthens fans' attachment to a celebrity. Behaviors that are randomly reinforced are likely to continue over the long term. Pop sensation Taylor Swift set a new standard for audience engagement when she responded directly on the social network Tumblr to a fan named Kasey who was going through an emotionally traumatic break-up. Swift responded to her with candor and empathy. Brian Spitzberg and William Cupach (2007) argue that interaction with celebrities is perceived as an interaction with a friend who happens to be famous. The possibility of access to a celebrity in this way – no matter how distant – can enhance the fan's self-esteem, leading them to imagine they are a kind of celebrity themselves.

A FINAL WORD

The web offers many different environments in which love and intimacy can be explored. On one end of the spectrum are the anonymous environments in which the other person doesn't know anything about you except the information you reveal. On the other end of that spectrum are sites like Facebook, where matchmaking starts with the exchange of a great deal of personal information.

The point at which people move from an online to a face-to-face interaction varies from one case to another. In some cases, people move immediately. Learning of a potential romantic partner on Facebook, for example, may lead to an in-person meeting that same day. In other circumstances, people live out their entire romance in the online world and do not wish to move it offline.

As always, there is an interplay between revelation and concealment, between fantasy and reality. These are the factors that make romance online possible, but they are also the very same factors that may make online pursuits of love (or something like it) so very fraught.

REFERENCES

Argyle, M. (1987). *The Psychology of Happiness*. New York: Routledge.

Ben-Ze'ev, A. (2009). Online relationships and the realm of romantic possibilities. In T. Dumova & R. Fiordo (Eds.), *Handbook of Research on Social Interaction Technologies and Collaboration Software: Concepts and Trends* (pp. 327–335). Hershey, PA: Information Science Reference.

Cotton, J. L. (1981). A review of research on Schachter's theory of emotion and the misattribution of arousal. *European Journal of Social Psychology*, 11, 365–397.

Dutton, D. G. & Aron, A. P. (1974). Some evidence for heightened sexual attraction under conditions of high anxiety. *Journal of Personality and Social Psychology*, 30, 510–517.

Ellison, N., Heino, R., & Gibbs, J. (2006). Managing impressions online: Self-presentation processes in the online dating environment. *Journal of Computer-Mediated Communication*, 11(2). http://jcmc.indiana.edu/vol11/issue2/ellison.html.

Goldman, D. (2003). Sex, lies and the internet. In J. Reid Meloy, L. Sheridan, & J. Hoffman (Eds.), *Stalking, threatening, and attacking public figures: A psychological and behavioral analysis* (pp. 287–321). New York: Oxford University Press.

Moshe, I. (2008). The impact of online surfer personality and motivation on choosing an avatar. MA Dissertation, Ben Gurion University, Israel.

Reis, H. T., & Shaver, P. (1988). Intimacy as an interpersonal process. In S. W. Duck (Ed,), *Handbook of personal relationships* (pp. 367–389). Chichester: Wiley.

Rempel, J. K., Holmes, J. G., & Zanna, M. P. (1985). Trust in close relationships. *Journal of Personality and Social Psychology*, 49, 95–111.

Rusbult, C. E. (1980). Commitment and satisfaction in romantic associations: A test of the investment model. *Journal of Experimental Social Psychology*, 16, 172–186.

Rubin, Z. (1973). *Liking and Loving: An Invitation to Social Psychology*. New York: Holt, Rinehart & Winston.

Sabatell, R. M. (1988). Exploring relationship satisfaction: A social exchange perspective on the interdependence between theory, research, and practice. *Family Relations*, 37, 217–222.

Spitzberg, B. H., & Cupach, W. R. (2007). Fanning the flames of fandom: Celebrity worship, parasocial interaction, and stalking. Paper presented at the annual meeting of the International Communication Association, San Francisco, May 23. http://citation.allacademic.com/meta/p169035_index.html.

Victor, A. (2015). The Ashley Madison data dump, explained. *New York Times* online, August 15. www.nytimes.com/2015/08/20/technology/the-ashley-madison-data-dump-explained.html?_r=0.

Wu, P. L., & Chiou, W. B. (2009). More options lead to more searching and worse choices in finding partners for romantic relationships online: An experimental study. *Cyberpsycholgy and Behavior*, 12, 315–318.

Yang, M. L., & Chiou, W. B. (2010). Looking online for the best romantic partner reduces decision quality: The moderating role of choice-making strategies. *CyberPsychology, Behavior, & Social Networking*, 13, 207–210.

Younger, J., Aron, A., Parke, S., Chatterjee, N., & Mackey, S. (2010). Viewing pictures of a romantic partner reduces experimental pain: Involvement of neural reward systems. *PLoS ONE*, 5(10): e13309.

4

VIOLENCE ON THE INTERNET

You kikes, it's just a shame the Germans didn't finish their job
— a "friendly" dialogue

I once entered a chat page that claimed to be about solving the Arab–Israeli conflict. The conversation that I found there seemed one-sided. The most active, vocal participants favored the Palestinian cause, and agreed with one another in short, sharp statements: "The State of Israel is a satanic state"; "Israel has no right to exist"; "All the Jews should go back where they came from," and so on. I tried to offer a bit of counterbalance, suggesting that Israel has rights and roots, and immediately felt like an intruder with all the searchlights trained on him. "You don't know what you are talking about," said a relatively polite commenter. "You kikes, it's just a shame the Germans didn't finish their job on you," said someone else. "We'll finish that job," said a third. A fourth responded with a reference to the dubious origins of my mother and father. For the first time in my life, I understood the feeling of facing a lynch mob in the public square. I'd run afoul of online aggression in the form of verbal violence.

In this chapter we will be discussing online aggression, and considering some important questions such as: What is aggression and how is it learned? Do people have to be anonymous in order to behave aggressively online? How do terror organizations use the Internet? We'll also be looking at the world of online hackers, asking what makes them tick and whether there are any true Robin Hood types. Finally, we'll be considering the issue of violence against women online. What is aggression and how is it learned?

Aggression is behavior intended to hurt another person. By definition it cannot be accidental. Selfish aggression is known as *utilitarian aggression* because it is perceived as useful to the aggressor in some specific way – resulting in a gain in social standing, for example, or the possibility of monetary profit. *Hostile aggression*, on the other hand, is aggression for the sake of aggression. Its purpose is to hurt the other party, not to bring any direct benefit to the aggressor (Rancer & Avtgis, 2006).

Aggression can be expressed as physical or verbal violence. A verbal aggressor may say disingenuously, "I didn't do anything violent." And while it's important not to lose the distinction between verbal insult and physical injury, it's also important to know that, while verbal aggression doesn't leave visible scars the way a bodily assault does, its results are sometimes much more severe. The psychological scars that remain from verbal violence may take far longer to heal.

So how do we learn to express aggression? Albert Bandura, one of the great social psychologists (see the nearby Mini-biography), dealt extensively with social learning (see Bandura, 1971). In 1961, he conducted a study that was, and still is, considered the most important attempt to understand the roots of violence in society. Bandura divided a group of children into two. One group watched an adult hitting and shouting at a bobo doll (a large inflatable doll that is weighted at the bottom so that, if tipped, it rights itself). The other group watched an adult calmly arranging some toys. Then Bandura put the two groups together into a room full of toys and dolls. The researchers began to irritate the children in various ways and recorded their reactions. The level of aggression was significantly higher among the children who had watched the adult act violently than among the other group. Some children even imitated the actions of the violent adult; they hit the dolls and shouted exactly as he had.

Bandura followed up with another experiment, this time dividing children into three groups. All three groups watched an adult displaying great aggression toward dolls. The difference was in the consequence for the adult. One group of children saw the aggressive adult rewarded with a snack – a sort of positive reinforcement for his actions. A second group saw the aggressive adult neither rewarded nor punished. And the third group saw the aggressive adult scolded and warned to stop – an explicitly negative response. Again, Bandura put all the children together into a room with toys and dolls, and again the experimenters irritated the children in various ways and recorded their reactions. The greatest aggression was displayed by the group that watched the aggressive adult receive a reward for his behavior. In the middle was the group who saw neither a reward nor a punishment, and the least aggression came from the group who had seen an unfavorable response to the aggressive man's behavior. It appears that the children who saw an adult's aggression rewarded tended to copy the behavior. Bandura thus concluded that seeing the adult being rewarded encouraged the children to imitate his behavior.

Bandura's research findings are relevant to our own times. In the spirit of Bandura, we may assume that children and adults who watch violent content online will tend to act violently, especially if it seems that the violent people are rewarded (with prestige, for example). If children see that violence pays, they will embrace it. On the other hand, if they see that violence incurs punishment, they are more likely to avoid it.

MINI-BIOGRAPHY: ALBERT BANDURA, AGGRESSION IS LEARNED

Born in 1925 and active for the past sixty years at Stanford University, Bandura began his career in psychology as a behaviorist – that is, assuming that a person consists of a mix of behaviors caused by environmental influences. Put very simply, behaviorism views a person as a sort of black box that responds to influences from outside, not from whatever may or may not happen inside it.

However, in the course of his work, Bandura decided that behaviorism is too simplistic. He contended that a person is the product of an interplay between environment, behavior, and psychological processes. In other words, a person is influenced by the environment but also influences it.

Bandura's contribution to psychology is broad-ranging and rich; one field in which his contribution is uniquely strong is the understanding of aggression. According to Bandura, most of our behavior – aggression included – is learned by watching and imitating others, rather than as a result of our own personal experimentation. As we observe the world and learn, we absorb rules that we apply not only in their original context but in additional situations as well. The process of social learning is neither passive nor technical: it's an active process in which the learner draws conclusions from incoming information.

Later studies based on Bandura's research showed that if a child experiences violence at the hands of his parents, he will respond aggressively toward other children, and even with insensitivity toward victims of violence (Simons, Wurtele, & Heil, 2002). Why does that happen? Because the child learns to reproduce the aggressive behavior of his parents, who treated him without empathy, and continues to imitate his parents despite his own experience of suffering. Researchers studying the influence of pornography found that, among men, exposure to violent pornography causes a significant increase in the tendency to act violently towards women. The explanation provided is that exposure to pornography caused the men to feel lenient toward violence against women, and encouraged the view that the women, the victims of violence, were "asking for it" and perhaps even appreciated the violence directed against them (Check & Malamuth, 1986).

HOW DOES THE INTERNET ENCOURAGE AGGRESSION?

The nature of the Internet means that online aggression takes place mostly on the emotional as opposed to the physical plane. However, it can sometimes result in actual physical harm to the victim, as in those chilling cases when an aggressor goads a victim into suicide. As we will discuss later on, many young people involved in cyberbullying combine online aggression with physical violence against their victim (Patchin & Hinduja, 2016).

Aggression is a primal human need, so it is no surprise that the first reported incident of Internet aggression appeared as early as the 1990s, when very few people had access to it. The incident occurred in a virtual community called LambdaMOO. Previously, this community had been considered a calm and friendly place, but with the entrance of the self-styled "Mr. Bungle" into the community, things began to change. Mr. Bungle was a hacker who knew how to break into the site's operating system and do things that the other community members could not. Mr. Bungle presented himself as a voodoo magician casting malignant spells on the other community members. He began exploiting his "evil powers," forcing himself sexually on the other avatars and using them as players in virtual sex activities against their will. This was the first virtual rape, and the females who were the victims of his attacks reported adverse long-term psychological effects (Dibbell, 1993). The incident demonstrated not only how easily the Internet could turn into a place of violence, but also the serious consequences of online abuse.

It is important to note that all the traits that make the Internet a unique psychological environment in a positive sense – the Magnificent Seven (see Chapter 1) – also work in the opposite sense and help make the Internet an arena for expressing violence. Here, we'll walk through the Magnificent Seven one at a time to get a better sense of how each one can contribute to online violence.

The *feeling of anonymity* and *control over level of physical exposure* give aggressors the impression that no matter what they do, no one knows who they are and no one can catch them. For them, it's like Dodge City with no sheriff. Protected by anonymity, attackers stand almost no chance of being punished, and, in most cases, the victim has no countermeasures available.

Attackers may operate within a community, as we saw in the "Mr. Bungle" example above, or they may exist as an organized community of aggressors who seek out certain types of victim (based on race, sexual orientation, and so on).

Because the rules of Internet behavior are rarely enforced, anarchic tendencies develop. Aggressors feel strong and victims feel helpless. And when it comes to taking action against violent websites, the situation is far from simple. Even if a violent site is removed from the net – a hate group that publishes racial slurs, for example – the people behind it can always find another server, somewhere in the world, where they can upload the same offensive content. There are very few prosecutions for this type of activity. This is partly because the legal issues are not clear, and taking action against the culprits contradicts the free spirit on which the Internet was built, not to mention that the sheer volume of such violent activities is almost impossible to police.

An exception is the war against the distribution of pedophilic materials online. Here, international enforcement organizations display unusual cooperation in their attempt to wipe out the phenomenon and have experienced some success. This is proof that, despite the complexities, cooperation among the various policing authorities is feasible.

High control over communications empowers the aggressor and emphasizes the victim's helplessness. The aggressors remain in their protected environment, and harass people, interfere with their peaceful lives, and threaten them via online communication. As soon as an aggressor senses some counter-development in the situation and no longer feels safe, then they simply disappear. The impression that online harassment will not result in negative consequences is well founded.

The aggressor's feelings of control derive partly from the fact that their antagonism is being conveyed remotely. Research has shown that when the belligerent act takes place from a distance, the aggressor tends to feel more uninhibited and may commit a more extreme form of violence against the victim (Haslam et al., 2008).

Being at a distance and in a safe environment, the aggressor may easily think of the other person as a sort of lesser human. All the more so, since they aren't fully exposed to the victim's feelings of pain and humiliation. If the aggressor wields technological superiority – better equipment, or better abilities – then the tendency to express antagonism is likely to be amplified. The case of Mr. Bungle, described above, is an example of this, since he was able to overpower his victims by means of his technological knowledge.

When the aggressor targets a victim that they actually know offline, this increases their control over the communication. In fact, the aggressor can refine the message and individualize it to hurt the victim more effectively. For example, if a group of high school students are targeting a fellow student known to be sensitive about her weight, then the aggressors will concentrate on that point in their cruel and hurtful barrage of comments and messages, thus targeting the victim's vulnerability to cause maximum pain.

Ease in locating like-minded people creates a hothouse for nurturing violence. On the Internet, the aggressor can find soulmates to share any particular hatred and any campaign of harassment – against people of any ethnicity or religion, for example. These friends will provide positive reinforcement, which acts as a reward for the violence expressed toward the hated group. Alliances tend to forge among aggressors, and individuals among their number may be seen as heroes defending their cause. Such alliances can magnetically attract loners who find no other groups to belong to. A newcomer needs only to echo the prevailing aggression, and the group responds with messages of welcome, with positive reinforcement, and with the offer of a sense of shared identity. Sometimes people express loyalty to a violent group simply because no other group has provided them with positive reinforcement. And with time, in order to strengthen that sense of belonging, such people may well become increasingly extreme in their views and behavior.

The Internet's *accessibility and availability at all times and places* is a key factor in making hate sites a reality, and the hate groups behind them provide a strong influence on aggressors. A group that gives the impression of being continually active – always engaging in dialogue, for example – provides aggressors with the sense that the group is always with them, and that they are expected to continually express their involvement. Thus, the aggressive component of people's identity will become increasingly apparent. The Internet's accessibility and availability also make it possible to attack at all times, without a moment's respite for the victim.

The Internet can actually be seen as an endless series of violent environments that are constantly active. For people with aggressive tendencies, the Internet provides endless places to express them, to learn new forms of violence, and to see violence rewarded. For such people, the Internet is a world of opportunities calling them to act.

Egalitarianism plays an important role here, too. In the online arena, frustrated people can find themselves metaphorically rubbing shoulders with others whom they would never approach offline. For example, when a politician posts an article on the web, any and every malcontent can respond to it mercilessly, in the crudest and foulest terms. Here, for once, an anonymous commenter can freely insult the office-holder and no one can interfere with their activities. Moreover, a person with extreme opinions, despite feeling marginalized in offline society, can feel equal and even valued as a member of a violent group. In fact many of the traits that make such people feel like outsiders offline actually enhance their standing in their online community.

Many hate sites are built on one of the most astute of website principles – *fun of web surfing*. Such sites include hate-based games, cultural heroes, chatrooms, and forums. They are completely hate-centered environments wrapped in fun, interactive ribbons. They create a user experience that draws web surfers back time and again. An example is a Nazi-friendly site (www.americannaziparty.com) that offers computer games in which the goal is to kill as many Jews as possible. Each Jewish man you "kill" is worth ten points, each woman fifteen, and each child thirty. The objective is, of course, to accumulate the most points.

IS ANONYMITY A NECESSITY FOR AGGRESSIVE ONLINE BEHAVIOR?

A number of years ago, a leading Israeli university asked me to teach a course on Internet psychology. The course was held in a lab in which each student had a computer with an Internet connection. The students were Jewish and Muslim undergraduates majoring in education, the majority being Jewish. My impression was that relations among the students were friendly. In one of the exercises that I assigned, I asked them to hold a discussion on the Arab–Israeli conflict. The discussion took place via the computer network, and, although everyone was supposed to be completely anonymous, one Arab student let her identity slip out. In response, she suffered a crude verbal attack from two anonymous participants. They scourged her with vulgar epithets such as "stinking Arab" and said "Go live in Jordan if you don't like it here."

I quickly stopped the electronic conference and we started to discuss what had happened. It was a severe incident; students had been deeply offended. I wanted to show that these two students had exploited their cover of anonymity in order to attack their fellow student. Here was a clear example of how anonymity can disconnect people from society's usual regulations. Most of the Jewish participants had disagreed with the political stance of the Arab students, but they had expressed their disagreement reasonably. The two students who chose to use verbal violence felt safe because they were certain that they could not be identified.

The fact that an aggressor feels protected on the Internet, and believes there is no chance of being caught and punished, is the primary root of aggression.

However, that invites the question: Are people aggressive online only when they are anonymous? The answer is complex. We can see a growing number of online groups in which people express themselves very aggressively. This has to do with group norms that are allowing and even encouraging aggressive expression. Since membership of online groups constitutes a significant part of our lives, they influence our individual norms accordingly. In this way, an individual group member, who would not normally behave in a violent manner, may adapt to group norms and start to express themselves aggressively. This type of behavior can often extend to a context outside of the group activity – for example, in face-to-face confrontations. However, aggressive expression "out in the open" (i.e., when people are identifiable) is for the most part restrained; most aggressive behaviors, especially the more extreme, are committed under cover of anonymity, when aggressors believe they will not be punished.

DOES THE INTERNET TURN GOOD PEOPLE BAD?

Can we conclude, then, that good people go online and start to act violently toward other people? The simple answer is, no. What we *can* say is that the Internet frees people from social restraints, and sometimes this can lead to the unleashing of previously suppressed belligerent tendencies. The Internet allows aggressors to ignore social norms, escape from their usual identities, and discard the masks they wear.

In that sense, it seems that the Internet has created paradise on earth for violent people. In this paradise, there are any number of ways to express violent tendencies: pedophilia, invasion of privacy, information theft, racial and religious incitement, intellectual property violations, and terrorism.

Truly, in an environment in which they feel they can do whatever they want, with no one to call them out or punish them for "inappropriate behavior," people with strong violent tendencies will behave in ways which are most natural to them. It does not, in other words, change people's nature.

It is also important to become aware that our definition of "good people" is in many cases based on the social persona people present in their public, offline, daily life. Some people are very good actors and behave in an impeccably politically correct manner. However, when they feel that they are in a protected environment, for example on the net, they will feel safe to express aggression against any group or individual. So, for example, the fact that someone is a professor of English at a distinguished university does not make them automatically someone who does not hold biased opinions about minorities. It is possible that this professor is using the Internet to find like-minded racist people and is actually expressing an extremely aggressive side of their character that is otherwise contained in the offline politically correct world.

Perhaps the closest the Internet comes to turning "good" people "bad" is that it may actually serve as a school for teaching violence to non-aggressive people. Bandura demonstrated that people learn aggressive behavior from watching aggressive acts that are rewarded, and on the Internet, this pattern is repeated constantly. The younger the user, the more likely it is that constant exposure to violence will impact their identity and behavior. Clearly, those people with more aggressive tendencies are more likely than others to seek out the violent aspects of the Internet, but this does not eliminate the likelihood that naïve people will also come under its belligerent influence.

WHO ARE MORE AGGRESSIVE ONLINE, MEN OR WOMEN?

It is accepted wisdom today that women are less aggressive than men, both online and offline. And it does appear that men tend to be more violent in situations in which they can express themselves directly, either physically or verbally. However, women tend to excel at indirect violence such as rumor-mongering, slander, cold-shouldering, and sophisticated rejection (Hinduja & Patchin, 2008). For this reason, women can be expected to express a level of online violence comparable to that of men.

Below, we discuss specific areas in which the Internet functions as a landscape of aggression. The areas we will consider are terrorism, hacking, and sexism on the net. Net-based violence directed against children is discussed in Chapter 5.

HOW DO TERRORIST ORGANIZATIONS USE THE INTERNET?

On the Internet, terrorists can find a wide-open playground for their activities (Weimann, 2006). I have no doubt that when the leading members of the US Department of Defense conceived the idea of the Internet, they never thought, even in their very worst nightmares, that come the twenty-first century, almost every kind of terrorist splinter group would boast its own website; that the many advantages offered by the Internet would be at the service of terrorists for organizing, planning, and executing their attacks on innocent people.

As well as aiding in planning attacks, the Internet also helps terrorist groups in a variety of other activities such as recruiting members, establishing communication, attaining publicity, and raising funds. Terrorist organizations direct their messages to various target publics over the net with great sophistication. We will discuss the three major target audiences: active participants, prospective recruits, and potential victims. Their primary target audience is the central core of active participants, who use the website as a platform for information about various activities. Messages are disguised by pre-agreed codes that even experts will find challenging to decipher.

By means of such encoded messages, a global terrorist network can operate with great efficiency. It can manage its affairs like an international corporation: the leader passes instructions to various operations officers around the world, and they pass instructions onward to their subordinates. Using the Internet for information transfer, the organization can create a compartmentalized network of active participants who cannot identify one another. Even if one cell is exposed, the damage to the overall network is minimal. Ironically, it was that very element of tactical compartmentalization that guided the US Department of Defense when it set up the Internet in anticipation of a doomsday scenario.

The second target audience of terrorist websites are prospective recruits. Some organizations, for example many Islamic terrorist groups, attempt to find supporters by opening Facebook groups and encouraging others to open similar online groups. Such groups target mainly young people who are at the stage of defining their identity and searching for meaning in life. Through these online channels, terrorist recruiters will work at providing answers to such young people in their search for identity and meaning. In fact, this kind of indoctrination not only provides answers, but also fulfills two other important human needs: belonging to a significant group and having an individual voice.

The terrorist group will attempt to persuade individuals from the general public of the merits of their ideology. The young person will receive access to a group that will provide them with a significant identity and cultural heroes. These heroes are likely to be religious leaders and activists who have inflicted pain on the enemy, for example suicide bombers. Such groups will use religious symbols that enhance identification with the fight and hatred towards the enemy. There are likely to be stories of heroism, of "brothers" who have fought bravely under the service of the Jihad, and special commemorative dates symbolizing remembrance of the infliction of pain and defeat on the infidels by the heroes of the Jihad. In this way, the fundamentalist terrorist group will become an important component in the young person's identity.

The online group is likely to encourage a process of group polarization; this is discussed at greater length in Chapter 6. Typically, in extreme Muslim groups that support terrorist activity, each group member wants to have an "independent" voice achieved by acts of violence, thus leading to a process wherein the group's collective voice will become increasingly radical.

It is interesting to note that, while at the first stage people strive to achieve an individual voice within the group, later, when they identify totally with the group, some of them are likely to behave according to the de-individuation process. Here, people in a group lose their self-awareness and adopt the norms of "crowd behavior."

When it comes to the impact of aggressive fundamentalist websites, here too it seems that the individual group member experiences a loss of self-awareness in favor of becoming part of the larger group. This loss of identity, particularly through religious messages, can reach the stage when the individual fully identifies with the group. This is likely to spill over from online radicalization to offline life, and the group member is likely to act with extreme violence against the outgroup (i.e., the targets), and be willing to sacrifice their own life in the pursuit of the enemy. This type of action may well lead to many injuries and loss of many innocent lives.

Some social groups aim to attract people from the community of true believers and transform them into the community of formal activists. Such a process is undertaken with extreme caution in order to ensure that spies do not infiltrate the organization. When new volunteers are recruited, enlisting people who do not fit the terrorist stereotype can be greatly advantageous, since such people can serve as couriers without immediately arousing suspicion. On the other hand, the less the new volunteer belongs to the community from which the terrorist organization sprang, or resembles a member of that community, the more will that person be suspected of untrustworthiness. So such a new volunteer will be performing under close watch, or will be assigned one task that will end in the grave.

In the era of social networking, many terrorist activities are actually carried out spontaneously. Having participated in the ongoing indoctrination process on social networks, people may decide on an impulse to perform an act of terror. In such a case, the weapon is likely to be an unsophisticated object, such as a kitchen knife, scissors or a even truck, as happened in France on Bastille Day 2016. This new type of terrorist is likely to have utilized information found online describing, for example, how to wield a knife in the most effective way to guarantee the death of the victim. Thus armed, the individual will seek a target. This situation is creating a huge challenge for the security authorities attempting to stop terrorist attacks because no matter how good the surveillance of known terrorist organizations, it is still hard to stop such acts when the aggressor is not a formal member of the terrorist organization.

The third target audience is potential victims, i.e., the group to be terrorized. In addressing this group, the objective of the terrorist organization is to arouse fear, and it publicizes its terrorist operations in order to "win" the target audience over to the idea that each of them, including their family and closest friends, is likely to be the next victim of a terrorist attack. This malevolent message is accompanied by an ultimatum to the target audience: if all its demands are not met, the terrorist organization will make good on its threats. The terrorist organization will try to show that, because it is fighting for absolute justice and has no mercy as it makes its way to that goal, it is unstoppable. It immortalizes its terrorism in well-concocted documentary films that deal with its successes in deadly operations, and by video documentation of enemy executions. In many cases, it will also try to challenge the credibility of the enemy leadership by presenting the "real truth" behind events (as distinct from the "false claims" of the enemy leaders and the enemy media coverage). Another way to psychologically attack the enemy is by publishing photographs of public figures from the target group – be it political leaders, army officers, and even soldiers – who were, according to the terrorists, involved in violence "against our people" and threatening them directly.

Examining the way in which terrorist organizations address their target audiences through various channels, we can see that most of them deploy a rather impressive public relations corps. Many terrorist organizations use social networks, chatrooms, forums, YouTube, and other net channels.

Terrorist organizations ignore the human aspect of their victims and use the psychological tool of dehumanization against the opponent, defining it as a group that has no human face. Thus, for example, after the attack on the Twin Towers and the Pentagon on September 11, 2001, Al Qaeda completely ignored the thousands of murdered people and chose instead to focus on the indignities that the Middle East had suffered, and was continuing to suffer, at the hands of capitalist America, and on the importance of the Twin Towers as a symbol of the decadence of the western world.

In addition, since a terrorist organization, like any group, requires funding, the Internet provides an excellent resource not only for raising cash but also for moving and laundering funds between different countries around the world. One of the most deplorable ways in which Islamic State militants raise money is by selling young girls using online applications.

WHO ARE THE HACKERS AND WHAT MAKES THEM TICK?

The term "hackers" refers to people who are experts in penetrating computer defense systems (Smith, Yurcik, & Doss, 2002). While this may appear to be a relatively new term, its roots lie with British intelligence during World War II, and efforts to break the codes of the famous Enigma machines – a series of electro-mechanical rotor cipher machines that were used by Nazi Germany to send secret messages of tactical importance. Many believe that the successful hacking of the Enigma codes played a critical role in the Allied victory. The term appeared again in the 1950s, when students at the Massachusetts Institute of Technology (MIT) challenged themselves to break into the university computers; they called themselves hackers. According to Steven Levy, in his book *Hackers: Heroes of the Computer Revolution* (1984), the ideology of the hackers was free access to information and he related it to the spirit of freedom associated with the 1960s. *Mr. Robot*, a US television series, features a young man trying to save the world using his amazing hacking skills. The positive image of hackers is actually reinforced by tales of those who have been arrested and imprisoned on such charges subsequently being offered well-paid jobs by the very companies whose computers they'd hacked into – this time to manage their security systems. Altogether, cultural confusion surrounds how to perceive hackers. Are they digital Robin Hoods or are they just modern digital criminals? You can consider this question from a personal perspective: maybe you enjoy watching pirated movies that were cracked by a hacker. Many people turn a blind eye to this issue. However, these same people would probably be very upset if their personal details were accessed by a hacker who then used their credit card information.

What all hackers have in common is their interest in penetrating computer sites; however, their motivations differ. Some are professional hackers whose desire is simply to make money; they seek to obtain people's credit card details or to steal and then sell information (on individuals or companies) acquired by hacking. Other hackers are motivated by ideology and some simply like a challenge.

The most prevalent ideology is protecting the common people from the mega-big companies which are out to harm them. One leading example of this ideology is the open web. Some hackers contend that the Internet represents a new world and that all information, music, and videos posted there are everyone's common property. For that reason they believe that protected sites should be invaded and information should be made public for everyone. Another hacker ideology is nationalist in nature. These hackers believe that they have a patriotic duty to attack the enemies of their nation state. They usually want to garner publicity for their deeds and will leave evidence of their activities behind them, for example by vandalizing the websites they attack.

Those motivated by the challenge see hacking as a call to engage in a contest, fight, or competition. The challenge can be external, that is, taking on a secured organizational website; and also internal, that is, in terms of measuring their own abilities. For some hackers, the challenge is to compete against evil powers – capitalist organizations and powerful entities such as Microsoft, Sony, or even the Central Intelligence Agency (CIA). The external challenge can also take the shape of a competition between hackers regarding who will be the first to hack a specific website. The internal motivation is more about trying to improve and challenge yourself as a hacker, in terms of the tasks you take upon yourself.

A friend of mine owns a large business with a very secure website. I asked him why he doesn't publicize his safeguards in order to deter hackers. He responded: "Yair, that would work in reverse. It would turn my website into a challenge for hackers all over the world. I'd be asking for trouble."

WHAT KIND OF PEOPLE ARE HACKERS?

Analyzing the personality traits of hackers isn't easy because, unsurprisingly, they are not the kind of people who usually come forward and volunteer to fill out personality questionnaires. Also, as we saw above, there are a whole variety of motivations behind hacking, so we can assume that there is no one personality profile. However, based on accumulated knowledge, we have a partial picture. Some evidence suggests a relationship between Asperger syndrome and hacking; there is also some evidence that links hacking to those with poor social and communication skills (Seigfried-Spellar et al., 2015). While this fits well with the existing image of hackers as extreme computer geeks, I believe that this represents only a very partial picture.

DO REAL ROBIN HOOD HACKERS EXIST?

Lisbeth Salander, the heroine of the fantastically popular *Millennium* trilogy (*The Girl with the Dragon Tattoo*, and so on) is a hacker motivated by a Robin Hood urge. (Note, many consider her to fall on the autistic spectrum.) Throughout the novels, Salander uses her knowledge of computers to break through the defense systems of various organizations and institutions that stand in the way of her relentless pursuit of the truth. For her most outstanding exploits against the forces of evil, Salander assembles a group of hackers whom she knows only from her online world and who are all portrayed as being extremely anti-social and generally uncommunicative offline, but who are willing to do whatever it takes for a fellow member of their legion. A hero like Salander, fictional or not, typifies the good hackers: the ones who protect the weak and the poor. These people call themselves "white-hat hackers." They try to differentiate between their own, ideologically based, hacking, which they believe is helpful to the development of the Internet, and the destructive, vandalistic behavior of others whom they contemptuously refer to as "black-hat hackers." "Anonymous" is one of the most fascinating of the white-hat hacker groups, and it has successfully built an entire framework of public relations to explain and support its activities. These hackers believe they are an elite group tasked with protecting the weak and doing battle on their behalf against gigantic companies that deprive the public of information it has a right to access. From every possible podium, they proclaim their sense of justice and their complete belief in the righteousness of their own path. Anonymous' central campaign is "free information for all," particularly in the realm of intellectual property, and they ceaselessly attack organizations in this field.

Today the credo of such ideological hackers – the so-called *hacktivists* – can be seen as rather naïve. But if they manage to fulfill their mission, they could seriously harm corporations and countries. A hacker could contend, for example, that no one has the right to collect payment for music, giving them the right to invade a music site and distribute its songs to everyone for free. If digital theft becomes the rule, then respected performers will be unable to support themselves and the hackers will have no stolen treasures to enjoy because there will be no treasures to steal. In other words, the hacker is profiting, for the time being, from the fact that not everyone is a hacker.

A response of sorts, on the part of the industry, is the economic model popularized by Apple's virtual music store, iTunes, where you can download the songs you like and the prices are cheaper than buying a CD. Apple reports increasing revenues year on year for this service, which is an example of what can be done to return economic viability to music making.

The WikiLeaks website bears comparison to the activities of Anonymous. It enables all Internet users to post confidential information they are privy to, generally in the course of their working life – be it with corporations or governments – on the web. WikiLeaks publishes all confidential information that reaches its hands because it believes in this approach to battling governmental corruption. The site's founder and editor in chief, Julian Assange, is an Internet activist. He was behind the coordinated November 2010 leak of hundreds of thousands of documents relating to the US involvement in Afghanistan and Iraq. The US authorities complained that the leak had seriously damaged both US security and interests. Anonymous decided to defend the interests of WikiLeaks and announced it would attack any organization that tried to harm the WikiLeaks site.

In 2013, when journalist and activist Edward Joseph Snowden leaked a large number of documents to *The Guardian* and *Washington Post* newspapers regarding secret surveillance of many people and organizations by the US National Security Agency, WikiLeaks saw itself as an ideological ally and published its unreserved support of Snowden. The leakers and hackers have wrapped themselves in the banner of a rather convincing ideology, so that sometimes the good guys and the bad guys can't be quite so clearly and confidently labeled.

WikiLeaks continues to see itself as the defender of true democracy and remains active, releasing confidential material on a regular basis. Here are a few examples. In 2015, WikiLeaks published documents showing that, over a number of years, the US National Security Agency (NSA) had spied on the French, German, and Japanese heads of state, including president, François Hollande and German chancellor, Angela Merkel. WiKiLeaks also revealed that the activities of the NSA were not limited to political spying, but also included observing business interests such as Mitsubishi and Mitsui in Japan.

These few examples demonstrate the ability of the hackers to make us aware of the far-reaching power of the US government, acting as an Orwellian "Big Brother." Various leaks revealed that the US government spied on many individuals, businesses, and governments with no clear justification. However, it also seems that WikiLeaks may well have damaged many interests in the western world, perhaps most notably in releasing information that may have compromised US secret agents and endangered the lives of their sources. The lesson here may be that we need to build a stronger institutional mechanism in the western world to protect ourselves from Big Brother, and, if we fail to do so, we cannot be surprised that websites like WikiLeaks will continue to exist and flourish as modern-day Robin Hoods.

DOES THE INTERNET PROVIDE A VENUE FOR AGGRESSION AGAINST WOMEN?

Sexism refers to prejudice against, and discrimination and stereotyping of people on the basis of their gender. It is usually directed toward women, tending to brand them as inferior or sex objects. Sexism clearly existed long before the advent of the Internet, but the net's unique characteristics allow it to flourish in that environment.

Journalist Steve Silberman revealed this phenomenon in the earliest days of the Internet. Upon entering an AOL chatroom under the name of "Rose," he immediately attracted a great deal of attention. Some of the messages he received were friendly, and others were aggressive and unpleasant. Silberman said later that he was shocked at the speed with which men became aggressive. It was a bad experience for him, which prompted him to make some conclusions about the overall attitude toward women on the net.

One theory relevant to the attitude toward women expressed on the Internet is the online disinhibition effect (Suler, 2004), which argues that anonymity allows people to abandon the restrictions and inhibitions they encounter in face-to-face situations. People strive for emotional catharsis online and this can take the form of being very affectionate and emotionally open to others. However, this behavior can very easily take a nasty turn and become aggressive in nature.

Online games often include sexualized characters. Female avatars are usually weak and submissive, rendered in unlikely physical proportions. It has been found that these games lead players to take on or reinforce an extremely sexist perspective, even in their offline behaviors. In some cases, this can go so far as to include normalizing sexual harassment and even strengthening a tendency to harass woman (Yao et al., 2010). As such, games tend to stereotype men as the aggressors and women as the victims; it will thus come as no surprise to learn that most games are male-dominated environments and as such further reinforce masculine norms.

Researchers Fox, Cruz, and Lee (2015) assessed the effect of Twitter, a social network used for short public posts, on sexist attitudes and behavior. Participants were asked to either share or write a sexist message; half of the participants carried out the task anonymously, and half were identifiable. In the second part of the experiment, the researchers asked participants to partake in a seemingly unrelated task – evaluating the suitability of male and female candidates for a specific job based on their résumés – to study the effect of writing the Twitter message. Results showed that anonymous participants reported greater bias against the candidates after tweeting than identifiable participants. Participants who composed sexist tweets reported a more hostile, sexist attitude and also ranked female job candidates as less competent, as compared to those participants who only shared sexist tweets. What makes this study very interesting is the fact that the experimental manipulation that occurred in an online setting had an effect outside of it (in candidate evaluation). It points out that sexist online dialogue can create sexist behavior offline.

Fox and Tang (2014) suggested that the expectation states theory can explain why people use gender stereotypes online. According to this theory, when a group comprising people from different backgrounds is tasked with an activity, it tends to import differences in status into the group even if such differences have nothing to do with the task to be performed. Members' status will determine who will assume dominant and submissive roles within the group. Imported differences in status might thus grant male members a more proactive role because they are perceived as being more competitive, stronger, more emotionally controlled and self-reliant. In this context, they are seen as being more suited than women to be in control of a group with a task to perform. Gender stereotypes are evident at every level of society and, based on these, group participants base their decisions about who should lead the group, who should be given more time to speak in discussions, and how much value should be given to the contribution of each group member. Consistent with this theoretical framework, Fox and Tang found that male participants who perceive every group in terms of a hierarchy in which they need to dominate, and who endorse inequality, superiority and prejudice among social groups, behaved in a more sexist way in online games. Their behavior was a reflection of their perception of woman as inferior and subordinate.

There are many men who treat women as equals and show them respect offline, but who display extreme sexism when hidden safely under the cloak of anonymity provided by the Internet. Unfortunately, sexist attitudes are evident across many Internet platforms, from joke sites to chatrooms and forums, even sports fan sites may devote a great deal of time to conversations that include remarks that are hurtful to women. It is, sadly, not at all surprising that the majority of complaints about online violence are filed by women.

This situation causes some women to present themselves as men in chatrooms and so on. Many women receive derogatory responses when they offer an opinion, a situation that is humiliating and hurtful.

A FINAL WORD

Web administrators must take responsibility for what is happening on their territory. Websites need to introduce more efficient reporting systems that can be used to counter aggression. Moderators should be less tolerant of racist, sexist, and any other form of discriminatory language that encourages hostility towards "others." Offenders should be warned and, if they repeat the behavior, expelled from the website. Some kind of quality standard mark should be introduced and awarded to websites that have a clear policy on the issue of aggression and uphold it. These measures, and more like them, would help create a more positive atmosphere and encourage increasing numbers of websites to do likewise. Furthermore, violence on the Internet should be controlled by legislation. Such legislation needs to be enforced by the companies behind the websites, whatever their size. It is the responsibility of the state to create laws that protect its citizens from violence, and this includes violence online. On a global level, nations should cooperate to tackle professional criminals who operate via the Internet.

Unfortunately, there is one large section of Internet users whom we have not yet touched upon, but who are victim to various forms of online aggression and violence – children. Exposure to Internet violence at a young age is known to affect children's emerging personalities, and their personal development. The issue of children and online aggression will be discussed at length in Chapter 5.

REFERENCES

Bandura, A. (1971). *Social Learning Theory*. New York: General Learning Press.

Check, J., & Malamuth, N. (1986). Pornography and sexual aggression: A social learning theory analysis. In M. L. McLaughlin (Ed.), *Communication Yearbook*, Volume 9 (pp. 181–213). Beverly Hills, CA: Sage.

Dibbell, J. (1993). A rape in cyberspace, or how an evil clown, a Haitian trickster spirit, two wizards, and a cast of dozens turned a database into a society. *Village Voice*, 21, 36–42.

Fox, J., & Tang, W. Y. (2014). Sexism in online video games: The role of conformity to masculine norms and social dominance orientation. *Computers in Human Behavior*, 33, 314–320.

Fox, J., Cruz, C., & Lee, J.Y. (2015). Perpetuating online sexism offline: Anonymity, interactivity, and the effects of sexist hashtags on social media. *Computers in Human Behavior*, 52, 436–442.

Haslam, N., Kashima, Y., Loughnan, S., Shi, J., & Suitner, C. (2008). Subhuman, inhuman, and superhuman: Contrasting humans with nonhumans in three cultures. *Social Cognition*, 26, 248–258.

Hinduja, S., & Patchin, J. W. (2008). Cyberbullying: An exploratory analysis of factors related to offending and victimization. *Deviant Behavior*, 29, 1–29.

Levy, S. (1984). *Hackers: Heroes of the Computer Revolution*. New York: Doubleday.

Rancer, A. S., & Avtgis, T. A. (2006). *Argumentative and Aggressive Communication: Theory, Research, and Application*. Thousand Oaks, CA: Sage.

Patchin, J. W., & Hinduja, S. (2016). *Bullying Today: Bulletpoints and Best Practices*. Thousand Oaks, CA: Sage.

Seigfried-Spellar, K. C., O'Quinn, C. L., & Treadway, K. N. (2015). Assessing the relationship between autistic traits and cyber deviancy in a sample of college students. *Behaviour & Information Technology*, 34, 533–542.

Simons, D., Wurtele, S.K., & Heil, P. (2002). Childhood victimization and lack of empathy as predictors of sexual offending against women and children. *Journal of Interpersonal Violence*, 12, 1291–1307.

Smith, B., Yurcik, W., & Doss, D. (2002). Ethical hacking: The security justification redux. *International Symposium on Technology and Society*. DOI: 10.1109/ISTAS.2002.1013840.

Suler, J. (2004). The online disinhibition effect. *CyberPsychology & Behavior*, 7, 321–326.

Weimann, G. (2006). *Terror on the Internet: The New Arena, the New Challenges*. Washington, DC: United States Institute of Peace.

Yao, M. Z., Mahood, C., & Linz, D. (2010). Sexual priming, gender stereotyping, and likelihood to sexually harass: Examining the cognitive effects of playing a sexually explicit video game. *Sex Roles*, 62, 77–88.

5

YOUTH AND THE INTERNET
ENTERING THE ENCHANTED FOREST?

The Internet is my home ... I'm in the center of the world ... I can do whatever, I can be whatever I want.

– anonymous young surfer

For today's children the Internet is an essential part of life, as natural as breathing. For young people, the online world isn't a place to be visited so much as an omnipresent, constant companion – at school, at home, and during leisure hours (Amichai-Hamburger & Barak, 2009). However, while they certainly know far more about the Internet than their parents, and probably spend much more time online, children and young people lack the sophistication to know how to navigate the hazardous terrain that comes with the online experience.

Of course, the Internet is used by children and young people in many positive and educational ways. For example, schools have developed fun ways to do what were previously mundane tasks, such as learning spellings or multiplication tables. In general, assignments are much more interesting when the pupil can see exciting films or images of the people, animals, and places they are writing about. Young people can volunteer over the Internet, take up causes, become more caring individuals. They can keep in touch with family and friends abroad. In fact, many elderly people have learned to Skype and joined Facebook to better keep in touch with the youngest members of their families. These are all wonderful additions to the young person's world.

Nevertheless, untethered, the Internet is likely to lead to hazards and danger. A world that seems to be one of equality, freedom, no boundaries, and significant empowerment may frequently become very dangerous. Although sometimes we may be tempted to ban our children from going online, we must recognize that the Internet is here to stay – for many young people, it forms the backbone of their educational, social, and leisure lives. With this in mind, this chapter is devoted to alerting readers to the complexity of and dangers inherent to the Internet and to providing an approach for healthy Internet use.

The starting age for Internet users is steadily decreasing while the average amount of time spent online is rapidly increasing (Mok et al., 2010). The advent of the smartphone – enabling Internet access and availability anytime, anywhere – is the main factor behind ever-increasing Internet usage by children. According to a Pew research study (Lenhart, 2015), 92 percent of US teens go online daily and, among these, 24 percent report being almost constantly online. As the Internet becomes a larger factor in the lives of people at progressively younger ages, the question of how Internet usage affects children and teenagers is becoming increasingly pertinent. This chapter addresses the online experience of children. It also considers a number of apposite questions, including: What are the pros and cons of Facebook usage for children? Does online pornography affect children and, if so, how? How does violence in online games affect children? What is cyberbullying and how may it affect children? And, finally, how do you identify if a child is addicted to the Internet?

After discussing these questions, and finding some answers, we will ask the fundamental question: How can parents regain influence over their children's online activities in the digital world? We will then provide the tools to answer it.

FROM THE PERSPECTIVE OF CHILDREN, WHAT ARE THE MAIN ADVANTAGES OF THE INTERNET?

From the point of view of children, surfing the net has a great many good things about it. (The myriad of attractions we discuss in this section closely mirrors the Magnificent Seven, which you may recall from earlier chapters.) On many websites, children can remain anonymous and experience no physical exposure. This gives them the ability to explore their identity and recreate themselves, free from the watchful eyes of parents and teachers. Even on those websites that do involve physical exposure, such as social networks, they still maintain a great deal of control over the way in which they present themselves. For teenagers, this suits the developmental stage that they are at, one in which they are highly sensitive to how they present themselves. So it feels particularly good to young people that, when online, they perceive a high degree of control over their self-presentation and interaction with others. They feel that they are in a physically protected environment, which allows them to take risks, often including visiting forbidden websites. The same feeling of control allows young people to interact with others whom they have never met offline, free from filters or suspicion, particularly because they know that, should things go wrong, they can always disconnect. Moreover, this online experience creates strong feelings of equality: the young person is equal to anyone; in fact, they are an authority figure, with infinite arenas for self-expression. As one such individual succinctly put it: "On the net, I am the media." On the net, a child can write feedback on a major speech given by the president, and in this arena, unlike in their life offline, what they write will not be assessed in terms of its quality and their age is irrelevant. The possibilities are endless. They can even put a short video clip on YouTube that will perhaps go viral, and they will be famous.

In addition, on the Internet young people can find similar others to share their hobbies and interests, which may be difficult to pursue in their physical environment. Forming relationships with people like themselves can help to build their self-esteem. For those in isolated locations, the Internet can offer their only opportunity to make like-minded friends. The traumatic experience of moving to a new location can also be tempered by the ability to stay in touch with their old group of friends.

The constant accessibility and availability of the Internet makes the online experience very real. It frequently feels to children that what is happening online is more significant than what happens offline. Their online groups are available all the time, providing them with role models and positive reinforcement. In this way the online world becomes very important to children's self-esteem. The Internet is also fun. One of the main aims of web designers is to please children and young people. These designers are aware that children give only a few seconds' attention to a website before deciding whether they like it or not, and, if they do like it, they will tell the "whole world" immediately. In this way, if the website succeeds in providing a great user experience to one young person, in a very short space of time, it may skyrocket in popularity. However, if the user experience is not special, a similar process will cause it to utterly flop. This kind of fierce competition is the main reason that websites continually seek to improve the user experience that they offer to young people. In addition, the Internet provides children with a sense of equality and, in keeping with the Web2 philosophy, the ability to get involved and seek to influence. When we put all of these positive components together, it seems clear that the Internet creates a fantastic, empowering environment for young people – one in which they reign supreme.

However, while this sounds all well and good, it is only part of the picture. The Internet, as we will discuss below, has many problematic and even dangerous aspects. Every pro has a flipside, and the seven factors that provide the potential to empower a child are also the cause of the serious harm that the Internet can inflict on that child. The feeling of total protection can fast become an illusion. Below, we will consider some of the Internet services and websites more carefully, and will identify the main hazards associated with them for children and young people. Since young people are the principal consumers of social networks, they will form our initial focus.

WHAT ARE THE PROS AND CONS OF FACEBOOK FOR CHILDREN?

Social networks allow users to interact with their friends on an individual level, within specific groups, and in a public manner. Currently the most popular social network is Facebook. There is a minimum age requirement of 13, but this is frequently violated and many children open their own Facebook pages at a much earlier age. I recently turned to Facebook to leave a birthday message for a 14-year-old boy, only to find that, according to the date of birth on his profile page, he was now 33. It seems Facebook use has become such an accepted and popular hobby that parents feel their child will be a social outcast if they are not part of the Facebook scene. Children generally believe that Facebook is a protected environment, where almost all potential advantages of the Internet exist. There, they enjoy their own private territory, over which they have total control, without interference from adults, particularly their parents. Moreover, they feel that they can control exactly how and what the world learns about them, for example they can choose which flattering photographs to upload, and which pieces of personal news to share. Running their social network activity is fast and easy, and they feel connected to their friends whenever and wherever they choose. It offers a great feeling of empowerment.

CHATBOX: TOMMY, THE WONDER CHILD

Tommy is 11 years old and already has 500 friends on Facebook. However, to be honest, he has actually met only forty or so of them face to face, and to be even more honest, aside from Facebook, he is not really in contact with them at all, because, after all, who needs to meet people in person when you have Facebook? Tommy lives with his mother and sister, but hardly sees them. His mother is involved in her work as a lawyer, while his sister is constantly busy with her friends. The family members do keep in touch with one another: they send each other WhatsApp messages and it works out pretty well. In his face-to-face social interactions Tommy is very shy, easily embarrassed, and prone to stuttering. On Facebook, however, he is very eloquent, doesn't stutter and never gets confused or embarrassed. He spends around five hours a day on Facebook. One hour at least is dedicated to updating his profile. He once spent over two hours editing his profile photograph until he was happy with the result. When he finally uploaded it, it garnered 400 likes, so his extra effort was worth it.

On a previous occasion, everything went wrong. Tommy uploaded a post, but received no likes or shares ... nothing at all. He hinted to some people to come forward and help him out, but the situation didn't change dramatically, so Tommy decided to remove the post. It was, he felt, the worst thing that could happen to anyone. In another more successful post, Tommy told his friends all about the nervous breakdown his sister had suffered following their parents' divorce. He revealed everything: the shouting, the crying, the weeks she spent in a psychiatric hospital. His sister was devastated, but that didn't really matter because he had received so many shares and likes. He was the king of Facebook for three blissful days.

Now, when he posts on Facebook, he feels an increasing degree of tension, particularly as he waits for responses. Will his friends feel excited? Will they like it? He feels that his entire self-worth is on the line. And then, when the first likes and shares begin to trickle in, he feels suddenly so alive and every-thing seems good, in fact amazing.

Somewhere, deep inside, Tommy knows that there are some people on Facebook who are more popular than him. He monitors some of them: they are better-looking than him, and their lives seem much more exciting than his. Sometimes this depresses him. A month ago he received a friend request from someone who looked nerdy, whom he did not recognize, and who had fewer than 200 friends. Naturally, Tommy did not approve him, as he was not about to put his own social standing at risk. When he looks at his friends' pic-tures, he sometimes wonders what they really look like. Would he recognize them if he met them in the street? He knows why this issue troubles him: he puts a lot of work into editing his images with Photoshop to make sure that he looks fantastic and he wonders if his friends on Facebook would actually recognize him if they met face to face.

Tonight, Tommy is going to meet one of his online friends: a boy called Jon. This will be their first face-to-face encounter, although Tommy knows that they have a lot in common, including their passion for collecting Star Wars memorabilia; in fact, they met through a site dedicated to this inter-est. Jon has invited Tommy to his home to see his collection. It is in a part of town that Tommy doesn't know well, and he has decided not to tell any of his friends and family – online or offline – about this meeting, so that it will be all the more exciting when he puts up a post about it later on. He is sure that he is going to have a great time and the whole thing is making him feel very grown-up.

Many young people spend a lot of time on Facebook and so it is not surprising that what they encounter there determines much of their self-image and self-esteem (Valkenburg, Peter, & Schouten, 2006). Anyone who puts up any content on Facebook will be anxious to know what the world thinks of it (and by extension, of him or her). Strategies have been developed, particularly among young people, to garner positive feedback (Ong et al., 2011). These include tactics such as adding catchy photos, keeping messages short, ending posts with a question, posting a message at a time when friends are usually online, and "hinting" to friends to give positive feedback. If the post does not receive what its "sponsor" defines as enough likes and shares, they may well remove it. Another very interesting component of the Facebook experience is the feeling that you are the center of the world. You write something and immediately get feedback in the form of "Wow," "Great," or "You're the king!" This feeling returns people to their earliest childhood, in fact to babyhood, when they believed that the entire world revolved around them. On Facebook, when young people write about their personal experiences, the "world" reacts immediately. This degree of focus on the self by young people is worrisome, as it is very likely to encourage narcissism (Mehdizadeh, 2010).

For most Facebook users, an integral part of the experience is the viewing of other people's profiles, comparing and contrasting them with their own. This activity may well lead to their experiencing a decline in their sense of satisfaction with life (Krasnova et al., 2013). Young people frequently forget or do not even realize that their friends are also busy with their own PR activities and thus the image they present is not a true reflection of their life or degree of happiness.

On Facebook nearly everything translates into numbers (in the form of likes, comments, friends, and so on), which is likely to cause young people, especially those who suffer from social difficulties, to create distorted perceptions of friendship. They may fail to understand the quality of true friendship and the importance of investing in it, and instead opt for a quantitative definition of such, where friends are collected like points.

HOW DOES ONLINE PORNOGRAPHY AFFECT CHILDREN?

Pornography refers to sexually explicit material that is primarily intended to arouse the viewer (Malamuth & Huppin, 2005, 315). Peter and Valkenburg (2009) defined sexually explicit material as content "that depicts sexual activities in unconcealed ways, often with close-ups with (aroused) genitals and of oral, anal, or vaginal penetration" (p. 408). A US study found that as many as 93 percent of boys and 62 percent of girls had been exposed to online pornography during adolescence. Boys were more likely to be exposed at an earlier age, and the number of young people affected appeared to be growing all the time (Sabina, Wolak, & Finkelhor, 2008). These percentages refer to intended and unintended exposure to pornography. Research demonstrates clearly that exposure to pornography at an early age can disturb the development of healthy sexual identity and create a distorted perception of relationships and gender roles (O'Hara et al., 2012). A child who is exposed to pornographic materials is likely to display problematic behavior, ranging from social withdrawal to sexual aggression towards other children (Valkenburg & Peter, 2011). Research has revealed that young people deliberately exposed to sexually explicit material are six times more likely to be sexually aggressive than those who are not shown such material (Ybarra et al., 2011).

Most parents would not want their children exposed to pornography, and indeed have no idea that such a thing could be happening, even inadvertently. In many cases, the child did not choose to be exposed to such material. Cultures in which sexual maturation at an early age is considered desirable grant young people who are sexually active a higher status. In such cultures an unofficial competition is likely to exist whereby young people will aim to score points based on how sexually active they are. Those wanting to demonstrate their early sexual development are likely to post explicit material as proof that they have "won" the maturity competition.

In other cases, young people might find themselves visiting pornographic websites by mistake. Some of these sites aim to trap young people by using misleading web addresses or placing misleading links in online games. What is troubling is the ease and speed of moving from what appears to be a protected website to a hardcore pornographic environment.

HOW DOES VIOLENCE IN ONLINE GAMES AFFECT CHILDREN?

Many violent games exist online, promoting values we would not wish our children (or anyone else, for that matter) to ascribe to. Although age restrictions apply to these sites, this situation is not monitored and young people are able to access them. Just to provide an indication of the level of violence contained in these games, here are a few examples. In the *Grand Theft Auto* series, if the male hero kills the prostitute after they have sex, he gets his money back. In *Mortal Combat*, fights end with disturbingly graphic visual images of the severed body parts of the enemy. Many of these games are very popular among young people, and those who do not play them are likely to feel like outsiders. This situation may lead them to try to improve their social status by starting to play these violent games. What effect is this type of play likely to have on children and young people? In terms of Bandura's social learning theory, described earlier, we can assume that they will observe and learn such violent behavior, and may apply it in the offline environment too.

Some people suggest that little difference exists between this type of violence and any other. Violence is a part of life and always has been, so why make so much fuss about its expression on the Internet? Research by Craig Anderson, from the University of Iowa, suggests that violent video games (the precursor to violent online games) have a stronger impact on the player than violence witnessed in films and television programmes (Anderson, 2003). According to Anderson, because games are much more active, real, frequent, and powerful, they have a greater impact on the player. Violence witnessed in films and television programmes is consumed fairly passively – at most, an observer might identify with a person committing a violent act. In contrast, video or online games encourage the player to not only identify with agents of violence, but also to transform their identity and project themselves into the game, uniting with the violent hero figure. His hand is their hand, his face is their face – the player *is* the violent hero. The Internet also provides immediate and powerful feedback in terms of sight and sound: a punch is accompanied by cracking ribs and pain etched on the enemy's face. Another important difference between films and television dramas and online games is the frequency of violence shown. In the former, violence is presented as part of a story, not the whole story. Online games can comprise only acts of violence. The reality factor is also significant. In the recording of martial arts matches on television, for example, the camera tends not to show the hit itself, but moves aside at the crucial moments. On the Internet, in contrast, the player can see the blow hitting the enemy and its impact on them; everything looks real and the details are not softened. To summarize, Anderson suggests that the online representation of violence is very powerful and it can have a very negative impact on young gamers. I would like to add one further factor to Anderson's observations: the Internet is available 24/7 and accessible from everywhere. Online games can thus be omnipresent and may easily dominate a child's life.

Some leading researchers have demonstrated very clearly how violent games affect the player. Rene Weber and his team from the University of California examined brain activity among children who played *Tactical Ops: Assault on Terror*, a violent game in which the player has to survive by killing as many people as they can. Weber, Ritterfeld, and Mathiak (2006) found that identical brain activity was demonstrated by children playing this game and people engaging in aggressive action. A Finnish research group (Wallenius, Punamäki, & Rimpelä, 2007) found that, among boys aged ten to thirteen, a strong connection existed between playing computer games and violence. As the boys played more aggressive computer games, they demonstrated increasingly aggressive behavior in their daily lives. This relationship was more pronounced among children who were not on good terms with their parents.

The creation and distribution of violent online games is a very lucrative business. For that reason, their promoters are running very sophisticated public relations campaigns focusing on research evidence showing that no relationship exists between playing violent games and violent behavior in real life. Such campaigns even point out the great advantages of these games, such as the improved coordination and spatial abilities of the players. The proliferation of such violent material will continue until such time as detractors organize campaigns against these companies.

IS IT POSSIBLE TO IDENTIFY A CHILD'S ADDICTION TO THE INTERNET?

While the Magnificent Seven (the seven factors contributing to the power of the Internet) play a role in all types of children's online behavior, they have a particularly powerful effect in relation to addiction. Online activity in general is highly addictive, because it allows the participant to experience a highly protected and significant sense of empowerment. It is also the case that almost every online activity can become addictive to certain people, from a young person tending a virtual farm to one logging onto Facebook every moment of the day. So, can parents tell if their child is simply having fun or engaging in addictive online behavior. Where is the border?

Griffith (1998) suggested that online addiction has six components: (1) *salience* – online activity dominates the child's cognitive life (i.e., the child seems to be thinking about it all the time) and behavior (i.e., the child does it whenever they can); (2) *mood change* – the child reports that they feel significantly different when online; (3) *tolerance* – the child needs increasing lengths of time to achieve an excited buzz online; (4) *symptoms of withdrawal* – the child seems to experience physical or psychological discomfort when Internet access is limited or stopped altogether; (5) *conflict* – the child seems to experience more conflict with friends and loved ones regarding Internet use; and (6) *wanting to go back* – the child strives to repeat their pattern of addicted online behavior.

One much more simple definition suggests that online addiction is a state in which the child's online activity is negatively affecting other important functions of life. If the child spends time with friends, helps at home, takes the dog out for a walk, does homework, wakes up on time to go to school, and generally functions well while there, it is clear that the Internet is not having a negative effect.

We, as adults, have to develop an awareness of our children's behavior. Offline, face-to-face interactions are crucial for the development of emotional intelligence (Altenmüller, Schmidt, & Zimmermann, 2013). Our ability to understand emotion and to transfer emotions depends on our ability to read body language and our motivation to understand other people. Living in a world that lacks face-to-face interaction results in a child with a very limited emotional repertoire, which is likely to lead to difficulties in understanding the emotional aspects of an interaction and with emotional expression in general.

ANOREXIA AND THE INTERNET

Adolescence is a stage of major physical changes and newfound awareness of the body. One of the most well-known and studied disorders affecting young people and their image of their own body is Anorexia nervosa, which is known to generally start during adolescence. Although more prevalent among girls, the gender gap is closing and more boys are starting to suffer from this condition. People who suffer from the disorder perceive themselves as being overweight, although objectively they may be extremely thin. This misperception is likely to lead them to adapt extreme eating habits, which left untreated may result in death. (Thus, Anorexia may be discussed under the rubric of violence, as ultimately it is a form of self-harm.) One of the major difficulties in treating this condition lies in countering the distorted body image of sufferers (Hsu, 1990). Several websites, for example "Pro Ana," appeal to those with anorexia as a community of "others." Rather than aiding in recovery from Anorexia, they actually support its perpetuation. They create a closed group culture that delivers, overtly and covertly, the message, *we are united against the world* or *we will protect you from the world*. Because the Internet is available anytime and anywhere, young anorexics may be constantly hearing messages supporting their extreme diet; moreover, these sites provide role models and positive reinforcement, even going so far as to offer advice about how to trick parents who wish to help their children recover. Such sites make attempts to change young anorexics' distorted perception very limited in scope. Interventions are especially difficult in cases where those suffering from a disorder resist outside help, such as anorexic girls who perceive their situation as being under control and maintain the illusion that they have the power to reverse it whenever they choose (Dias, 2003).

Countering these websites is not easy because they can move from one place to another. They also present a very sophisticated agenda, in that they claim to provide a non-judgmental environment for anorexics as a "lifestyle choice."

WHAT IS CYBERBULLYING AND HOW DOES IT IMPACT CHILDREN?

Cyberbullying has been defined as the perverse and inappropriate use of electronic means, such as the Internet, to repeatedly assault a person, who is usually defenseless, in order to harm them and cause damage to their reputation (Smith et al., 2008). Here, we focus on cyberbullying among children, although adults can also become victims and perpetrators. Cyberbullying can happen in a number of ways, including sending insulting or threatening emails, distributing humiliating video clips of victims, and creating online groups with the aim of targeting victims. It is estimated that at least 30 percent of children and young people have been victims of cyberbullying (Vandebosch & Van Cleemput, 2009) – a frightening statistic. It is safe to assume that this percentage is actually even higher as a result of increased smartphone usage on the part of children and young people. Also, cyberbullying is widely underreported.

It has been posited that the main reason for bullying is frustration (Hoff & Mitchell, 2009). Some researchers believe that bullies' frustration arises out of their inability to cope with the challenges of life, or from having unattainable dreams and aspirations. This causes them to direct their anger, frustration, and aggression at a convenient target. In a situation like this a child who is weak and can be associated in some (even distant way) with the frustration felt by the bully is likely to become a target (Wright & Li, 2012). Pleas from the victim to stop the bullying have the same effect as blood for a shark, and usually provide the aggressor with an even greater sense of satisfaction and reinforce the aggressive act. If there is no reaction from the victim, and the aggressor does not gain positive reinforcement, the bullying may in fact stop.

In many cases, the online aggressor is also likely to be an aggressor offline (Vandebosch & Van Cleemput, 2009). However, in other cases, a person will be non-aggressive in their offline life, but under the cloak of protection granted by the Internet will feel free to express significant antagonism. It is sometimes the case that bored children looking for some fun will start to bully someone as a game. It is also important to realize that the borders between offline and online activity may be blurred. The bully might humiliate the victim in the offline world, take a video clip of the act, and put it on the net.

Vandebosch and Van Cleemput (ibid.) examined the personality profile of online victims of bullying. They report that, as with aggressors, the personality profile of a victim is very similar to that of the typical victim offline. Typically, it is a child who is socially rejected and who has poor social skills. Their need for love and affection is strong and initially they may indeed be seeking the friendship of the aggressor. When the bullying starts they will often beg for mercy and try to please the aggressor, a scenario that often makes the situation worse.

Some significant differences exist between cyberbullying and offline bullying. First, traditionally bullying was limited to a specific environment such as school, but at home the victim felt safe. In the digital era, this is no longer the case. On the net there is nowhere to hide. For parents it can be hard to fathom that the bullying may be continuing while they are actually sitting with their child, while that child looks at their mobile phone. Second, cyberbullying might never end. The tools are always available and, even if the bullying stops, it can very easily be resumed. Third, the aggressor feels protected and therefore will lack inhibition. Fourth, it is very easy to transfer an individual act of bullying into a group campaign whereby the victim will feel surrounded by hatred and unable to address it. In fact, similar to traditional bullying, many others may be frightened of the bully and decide to join their group because it is safer to be on the inside than on the outside – an act that further isolates the victim, who will never be allowed in.

Unfortunately, for many reasons, children are unlikely to complain to their parents. Foremost among them is that the child believes (often correctly) that the first action of the parents will be to take away the means through which the bullying is received – the mobile phone, tablet, or computer. Sometimes young people are driven to the point of suicide as a result of cyberbullying. In fact, the children most likely to commit suicide are the hybrid cyber "bully-victims," those who have been both victims and bullies (Aboujaoude et al., 2015).

It is almost impossible to understand the motivation behind them, but some companies have actually developed applications to enable children to write nasty messages to people while remaining anonymous. This encourages the release of all inhibitions and can create terrifying campaigns of intimidation. It is hard to believe that the developers of these applications have not realized their lethal potential, or, perhaps worse, they simply do not care.

Most children respond passively when they encounter a campaign of bullying on their social network. As parents and educators, we have to make children and young people aware that their passivity makes them part of the problem. Moreover, ignoring the situation allows the aggression to spread and may make them vulnerable to bullying themselves. It is important that young people understand that others are likely to join them if they take action against the bully. It is vital that children are educated about how to deal with cyber-bulling. They must also be encouraged to report it to their parents, teachers, and those responsible for punishing the perpetrators.

HOW CAN PARENTS REGAIN INFLUENCE IN THE DIGITAL WORLD?

According to Bowlby's theory of attachment, a positive connection between parent and child is necessary for the healthy development of the latter. Parents who are present, physically and mentally, and provide their child with protection and encouragement are likely to raise a child who is confident and feels a sense of control over her own life. When this is the child's early experience, she will allow herself to explore her environment knowing that if she encounters danger, her parents are there to protect her. The secure environment will help her to develop into an adult who trusts the world, enabling her to develop healthy social and romantic relationships (Simpson, 1990).

MINI-BIOGRAPHY: JOHN BOWLBY

Edward John Mostyn Bowlby (1907–1990) was a psychologist and psychiatrist best known for his research into attachment formation and his development of attachment theory.

Bowlby was born in London to an upper-middle-class family. His father was a baronet and a member of the king's medical staff. From his birth, Bowlby was exposed to the very strict upbringing typical of his class. His main caregiver was his nanny, Minnie. At that time mothers were instructed to be very careful not to spend too much time with their children, and not to be too warm towards them, because doing so would spoil them. Thus Bowlby's mother spent, at most, an hour a day with him after tea was served. His father was at home only on Sundays and spent almost no time with his children.

When he was only four years of age, Bowlby's nanny died; he later described this event as one of the most difficult moments of his life. At the age of seven, he was sent to boarding school. This upbringing may well explain why he chose to focus on maladapted children, and devoted much of his professional life to the understanding of healthy attachment.

Bowlby started his academic life studying medicine and progressed to become a psychiatrist, psychoanalyst, and an expert in child development. His attachment theory laid the foundations for future developments in this field, and is considered to be one of the most validated and far-reaching theories in its ability to explain human behavior.

Despite our great love for our children, many of us do not spend enough time with them. Work can consume our lives and we may convince ourselves that at some point in the future things will be easier and we can connect with our children then (on the presumption that said children still want to be connected with!).

As a solution to this social reality, the notion of "quality time" has evolved. According to this idea, it is possible to create a strong relationship with a child, even when time is limited, if the parent can stay in the here and now listening to, playing with, and responding to their child in a meaningful way. Grandparents and grandchildren often have a very close relationship because they spend valid time together. Unfortunately, the fast-paced, multi-tasking environment that many of us inhabit may mean that we have almost forgotten how to truly be with our offspring, without texting or taking urgent calls from work.

The constant bleeping of an electronic device during time spent with a child conveys the message "You are less important than my work or my emails." In the modern world parenting is ascribed very low status, and people thus tend to validate their sense of self-esteem from societal feedback on their work. Therefore, time spent with children can feel like a conflict of interests or even a form of drudgery coupled with exhaustion (negotiating with a two-year-old over the color of his cup may well be less rewarding, and more exhausting than drawing up a water-tight legal contract, for example). Spending quality time with your children is a state of mind; it demands real presence. When such time is constantly disturbed by a cellphone, you are not truly with your children, just as you would not be fully involved in a movie if you kept checking your phone. When a parent's time with their children is fractured, those children become gradually aware that their parent is not fully present in their life and then create their own world and are no longer interested in sharing it. This is one of the reasons why parents have lost touch with what happens to their children online. Teenagers are certainly more secretive by nature, but younger children are not unless they feel a sense of alienation from their parents.

HOW CAN WE PARTAKE IN OUR CHILDREN'S ONLINE LIVES?

Remaining aware of your child's online experience is neither simple nor straightforward. The Internet, unlike television, has no menu of programs on offer; there is no one in charge; and it is not clear with whom, if anyone, one can lodge a complaint. Children frequently have a greater understanding of the Internet than their parents. Moreover, since schools adopted the Internet as a pedagogical tool it is difficult to ascertain if children are using it to complete homework or for other, possibly sinister, purposes. Standing over a child while they use the Internet is not conducive to family harmony, and banning or disconnecting the Internet as a punishment for negative behavior may lead to difficulties at school. What is a concerned parent to do?

Every change process starts with taking responsibility for the relevant issue, including the parent–child relationship. This is not a static situation – if it is neglected, it will decline and disintegrate even further. Furthermore, we cannot transfer the responsibility for our children's behavior and experience on the Internet to their school or any other social agency (although we can recruit others to our "team"). Two main approaches to parenting are *authoritarian* and *authoritative* (Baumrind, 1991).

The authoritarian parenting style involves the parent establishing goals and roles. It is based heavily on regulations and punishment.

The authoritative parenting style places the child in the center. The parent has demands and standards, but is also responsive to the child's abilities and needs, and takes into account the child's level of development. The relationship between authoritative parents and their offspring is characterized by warmth and acceptance.

Authoritarian parents are likely to set up clear, specific rules for their children, including time on the Internet. Parents following this approach employ a variety of tools, including the use of protective software that allows children online access to "clean" websites only, or filters that block certain content such as violence and pornography. Parents are likely to demand that their children use the computer only in public areas of the house. The children will be unlikely to be allowed to use their smartphones in their bedrooms. In addition, such parents are likely to try to monitor the age at which their children join Facebook and to delay it for as long as possible. They will probably insist on being a friend on Facebook so that they can carefully monitor what their children are doing and constantly examine their online history. In some cases, authoritarian parents are likely to spy on their children with hidden cameras.

The main problem with the authoritarian approach is that it is power-based. As the children get older, they are likely to try to deceive their parents. As the children develop more and more sophisticated techniques, parents will gradually know less and less of what is really happening to their children online. Also, maintaining the authoritative style is demanding for the parent. It requires a degree of involvement in their children's life experiences offline and online. While it may be effective for young children, for older children it is likely to cause antagonism and disrespect.

The rules applied in the authoritative household may well be identical to those in the authoritarian household; however, because the process of adhering to them is different, the outcomes will be too. In the authoritative home, the challenge is to grant responsibility to the children for their Internet usage, according to their stage of maturity. The children thus understand and accept the offline and online risks and see them as their own challenges. The children will receive an explanation for their restricted Internet access and be part of ongoing discussions on the subject. From an early age, the parent will attempt to explain the need for careful and responsible use of the net, for the children's own good and to protect them from the many hazards out there. In fact, in such households many of the ideas for regulating Internet access will come from the children themselves following family brainstorming sessions on how to stay safe online. And because these ideas have come from the children, they "own" them and so will stick to them. It is important to stress that such rules are not a sign of a lack of trust, and as the children grow older they will be expected to take more responsibility for their own activities online. Adapting rules to the age of your children is the key to success here: treating an adolescent as you would a small child is a recipe for failure, anger, and deceit.

CHATROOM: THE SAVVY YOUNGSTER

Tim is ten years old. He is an Internet native. He does whatever he feels like and his parents know very little about what he does. Two years ago he asked his father if he could join Facebook; his father objected strongly, but was unable to stand up to the pressure placed on him by his son. Tim asked his friends to tell his father that they were already on Facebook and that, if Tim didn't join, he would be excluded from his peer group. In order to protect Tim, his father insisted on being Tim's friend on Facebook so that he could watch what went on. Tim agreed, but what his father did not know was that Tim blocked his ability to see much of what Tim was doing online. Although Tim's father had used software to limit Tim's access to certain sites, and to report on his online history, it actually took a mere three minutes for Tim to bypass the software and block its ability to follow him. His father will probably never know about the problematic and dangerous websites Tim is visiting. He is oblivious to the problem, as he studiously goes through the reports on Tim's online activities.

The basis of the authoritative approach is open communication with one's children. And this is an important link to the quality time described earlier in this chapter, because, without it, open communication is not possible. Real communication is a long-term investment, and it is possible only through an ongoing process of listening and building trust. Open communication will increase the likelihood that your children will come to you when they encounter a difficult situation on the net.

It is possible to see our relationship with our children as an emotional bank account (Covey, 1989). In this emotional bank, everything we do with our children is either a withdrawal or a deposit. When we do not meet our obligations toward our children, we run up an overdraft. The question is, what do we do to ensure a significant deposit rests in their bank account? Following these steps is the answer:

1. Set up a regular, fixed time for you and your children to spend time together.
2. Do not let technology disturb you. Turn off all smartphones, tablets, laptops, and so on.
3. Be present both physically and mentally. Really listen to what they say. Be non-judgmental. Ask only clarifying questions, reflect their answers back to them, and do not discuss your personal history. Ensure the focus is completely on them.

Remember, learning how to spend quality time with your children is a process. If the first meeting of this kind takes place after a long period of withdrawal from your children's bank account, they are likely to think that they are in trouble because they have received only negative feedback from you recently. So build a pleasant atmosphere around the meeting and set realistic expectations. Start asking your children about different aspects of their lives. Encourage them to talk about their studies, friends, hobbies, and, of course, what they're doing on the Internet. Try to understand the difficulties and challenges they encounter from their perspective. Strive to understand their personal experience. Every piece of listening you do makes a significant investment in their bank accounts. Let your children lead the conversation. They may well be very hesitant initially and may take time to open up. Remember to be a good listener; look into their eyes, use positive body language, and provide vocal feedback. The most important thing is not to be judgmental and to resist the urge to provide instant answers. Remember to guard against an automatic reaction to what they say, since it is likely to be negative. Such a response will close the cycle of communication and entirely miss the point of this new process. Instead, try to understand their experiences. See this conversation as an opportunity and a door they are opening to their world. Try to see the world through their eyes, and listen carefully and attentively. Ask questions for clarification, but without a trace of judgment. When you phrase questions properly, the child will open up to a greater degree. If they describe challenges they are trying to deal with, try to work with them to reach a solution. Remember not to take the lead. Let them come up with a variety of ideas. Analyze them carefully together and try to let them reach a solution. Slowly and gradually your interpersonal connection will improve significantly. Eventually, they are likely to reach out to you with a problem they are facing without you having to encourage them to do so. Also, be aware that your children may express pent up anger towards you, and be prepared to listen to criticism. Try not to be defensive: there may be a lot of truth in what they say. Your job is to listen. Sometimes you may have to tell them that you want to consider their comments for a few days before responding.

WHAT INTERNET TOPICS SHOULD YOU DISCUSS WITH YOUR CHILDREN?

When a sense of trust has developed between you and your children, you can then instigate discussions about their online behavior. For example, as the children mature you can bring up issues such as the amount of time spent online, introducing outside sources to the discussion such as psychological and medical evidence on the benefits and hazards of Internet use. Let the children relate personally to the information and come up with their own thoughts. Another example is the issue of privacy. Explain to your children the psychological factors relevant to young people's behavior on Facebook, such as the issue of revealing private information. Examine with them the short- and long-term results of putting private information online. It is also extremely important to work with your children on the definition of friendship and what it means to be a friend and have a friend – the differences between the first circle of intimate friends, relationships which require face-to-face interaction, and the peripheral circle of friends, those whom they meet only occasionally.

Parents need to encourage their children to go out and meet friends face to face, to join a youth movement, to develop their interests and hobbies, to volunteer. In this way, and crucially, their children's self-esteem will be created from different sources. When children develop and feel good about different facets of themselves, they are able to maintain more stability. Should they experience a challenging or an unhappy time in one aspect of their life, say in school, they have other environments through which to compensate. We need to teach our children how to cope with social pressure. This can be done through role-play, where we can act out different scenarios typical to the Internet. For example, what to do when our friends on Facebook start to bully another friend.

We, as adults, need to understand the feeling of empowerment children can experience on the net. When we tell our children not to enter a problematic website, we have to offer an alternative website. For example, in the online gaming arena, it is highly recommended that children do not play on the free websites with all-inclusive access, because we have no idea with whom they are playing and what advertisements they are being exposed to. We have to direct our children to the high quality game websites where they are protected – even if such websites require payment. The best websites check out who is joining and thus protect our children. In this way, we can demonstrate to our children that we want to help them, guide them, and allow them access to the best of the Internet, but without the dangers. We have to explain to our children that providing personal details puts them in real danger. When we forbid our children to meet up alone, face to face, with other "kids" they meet online, we need to explain the reasons to them, in accordance with their age and understanding. If, as parents, we use only our authority with no explanation, we are likely to create an even stronger motivation in our children to meet their online "friends" in person. We also need to be able to empathize with our children's sense of frustration and disappointment. Crucial to setting boundaries is the ability to empathize, but not necessarily agree, with children's views on the matter. In addition, we have to help our children develop critical thinking skills according to their age and cognitive abilities. Children have to be able to detect attempts to influence their attitudes and behavior.

A FINAL WORD

For young people, the dichotomy of the online world is particularly marked. This mixture of positive and negative can be very confusing. For this reason, mastering the online landscape and being aware of its hazards is absolutely vital. Just as we teach children the rules for safely crossing the road and, later, how to be safe drivers, so we should be teaching Internet awareness. Of course, when it comes to teaching web safety, the situation is more complex since most young people believe they know much more about the technology than their teachers and parents. Moreover, when you consider that risk-taking and learning social norms from one's peers is a natural part of teenage development, the whole situation only grows in complexity, compounded by the total and absolute freedom of information (be it bomb-making or how to commit suicide), which is the credo of the Internet. All these elements present serious challenges to those trying to keep young people out of danger online.

Being present in our children's lives is the best guarantee that we will be able to help them. Equally important, we need to remember that our actions speak much louder than any of our admonishments, and so if we ourselves do not control the amount of time that we are online or the type of websites that we visit, we cannot be surprised when our children follow suit. The norms of restrained and responsible use of technology start with the adults in the household.

REFERENCES

Aboujaoude, E., Savage, M., Starcevic, V., & Salame, W. (2015). Cyberbullying: Review of an old problem gone viral. *Journal of Adolescent Health*, 57(1), 10–18.

Altenmüller, E., Schmidt, S., & Zimmermann, E. (2013). *Evolution of Emotional Communication: From Sound in Nonhuman Mammals to Speech and Music in Man.* Oxford: Oxford University Press.

Anderson, C. A. (2003). Violent video games: Myths, facts, and unanswered questions. *Psychological Science Agenda: Science Briefs*, 16, 1–3.

Amichai-Hamburger, Y., & Barak, A. (2009). Internet and well-being. In Y. Amichai-Hamburger (Ed.), *Technology and Well-being* (pp. 34–76). Cambridge: Cambridge University Press.

Baumrind, D. (1991). The influence of parenting style on adolescent competence and substance use. *Journal of Early Adolescence*, 11, 56–95.

Bowlby, J. (1973). *Separation: Anger and Anxiety, Attachment and Loss*, Volume 2. London: Hogarth Press.

Dias, K. (2003). The Ana sanctuary: Women's pro-anorexia narratives in cyber-space. *Journal of International Women's Studies*, 4, 31–45.

Griffiths, M. D. (1998). Internet addiction: Does it really exist? In J. Gackenbach (Ed.), *Psychology and the Internet: Intrapersonal, Interpersonal, and Transpersonal Implications*. New York: Academic Press.

Hsu, L. K. G. (1990). *Eating Disorders*. New York: The Guilford Press.

Hoff, D. L., & Mitchell, S. N. (2009). Cyberbullying: Causes, effects, and remedies. *Journal of Educational Administration*, 47, 652–665.

Krasnova, H., Wenninger, H., Widjaja, T., & Buxmann, P. (2013). Envy on Facebook: A hidden threat to users' life satisfaction? Proceedings of the 11th International Conference on Wirtschaftsinformatik, Leipzig, Germany, pp. 1–16.

Lenhart, A. (2015). Teens, social media and technology overview. www.pewinternet.org/2015/04/09/teens-social-media-technology-2015/.

Malamuth, N. M., & Huppin, M. (2005). Pornography and teenagers: The importance of individual differences. *Adolescent Medicine*, 16, 315–326.

Mehdizadeh, S. (2010). Self-presentation 2.0: Narcissism and self-esteem on Facebook. *CyberPsychology, Behavior, and Social Networking*, 13(4), 357–364.

Mok, D., Carrasco, J. A., & Wellman, B. (2010). Does distance still matter in the age of the Internet? *Urban Studies*, 47, 2747–2783.

Ong, E. Y. L., Ang, R. P., Ho, J. C. M., Lim, J. C. Y., Goh, D. H., Lee, C. S., et al. (2011). Narcissism, extraversion, and adolescents' self-presentation on Facebook. *Personality and Individual Differences*, 50, 180–185.

O'Hara, R. E., Gibbons, F. X., Gerrard, M., Li, Z., & Sargent, J. D. (2012). Greater exposure to sexual content in popular movies predicts earlier sexual debut and increased sexual risk taking. *Psychological Science*. DOI: 10.1177/0956797611435529. http://pss.sagepub.com/content/early/2012/07/18/0956 797611435529.

Peter, J., & Valkenburg, P. M. (2009). Adolescents' exposure to sexually explicit internet material and notions of women as sex objects: Assessing causality and underlying mechanisms. *Journal of Communication*, 59, 407–433.

Sabina, C., Wolak, J., & Finkelhor, D. (2008). The nature and dynamics of internet pornography exposure for youth. *CyberPsychology & Behavior*, 11, 691–693.

Simpson, J. A. (1990). The influence of attachment styles on romantic relationships. *Journal of Personality and Social Psychology*, 59, 971–980.

Smith, P. K. Mahdavi, J., Carvalho, M., Fisher, S., Russell, S., & Tippett, N. (2008). Cyberbullying: Its nature and impact on secondary school pupils. *Journal of Child Psychology and Psychiatry*, 49, 376–385.

Valkenburg, P. M., Peter, J., & Schouten, A. P. (2006). Friend networking sites and their relationship to adolescents' well being and social self-esteem. *CyberPsychology & Behavior*, 9, 584–590.

Vandebosch, H., & Van Cleemput, K. (2009). Cyber bullying among youngsters: Prevalence and profile of bullies and victims. *New Media and Society*, 11, 1349–1371.

Wallenius, M., Punamäki, R., & Rimpelä, A. (2007). Digital game playing and direct and indirect aggression in early adolescence: The roles of age, social intelligence, and parent–child communication. *Journal of Youth and Adolescence*, 36, 325–336.

Weber, R., Ritterfeld, U., & Mathiak, K. (2006). Does playing violent video games induce aggression? Empirical evidence of a functional magnetic resonance imaging study. *Media Psychology*, 8, 39–60.

Wright, M., & Li, Y. (2012). Kicking the digital dog: A longitudinal investigation of young adults' victimization and cyber displaced aggression. *CyberPsychology, Behavior, & Social Networking*, 15, 448–454.

Ybarra, M. L., Mitchell, K. J., Hamburger, M., Diener-West, M., & Leaf, P. J. (2011). X-rated material and perpetration of sexually aggressive behavior among children and adolescents: Is there a link? *Aggressive Behavior*, 37, 1–18.

6

GROUPS AND LEADERS

I never felt I belonged. I always felt that the real social life was happening somewhere else ... Since I found the Internet I'm flourishing. I feel there are many people like me; we are interacting all the time. At last, I belong.

– an anonymous net user

Imagine you find yourself in a quiet corner, with your phone turned off, and a few moments to concentrate. If you were to consider what makes you who you are, what might you come up with? Try to define yourself. If you had to describe yourself to someone in five sentences, which start with "I am...," what would you say?

WHAT DID YOU SAY?

I assume that, like most people, you defined yourself partly by relating to groups you belong to. Some of the groups might be professional (I am part of my medical association); some of them may be connected with your hobbies (I am a Manchester City fan; I am a member of a book club); where you live (I am a citizen of Italy), and so on. Social belonging is a very important part of our identity. During a regular day different aspects of our social identity are likely to be activated many times depending on the contexts we encounter.

You could be aware of your group identity as a teacher, prompted by attendance at a professional conference. Watching the New York Yankees could remind you of your identity as a fan.

This chapter will explain the components of our membership of groups, either online or with an online component. We will be asking many important questions such as: How does such membership influence our individual identity? To what extent are groups relevant to the online experience? Can we act simultaneously as both individuals and group members online? We will also be examining group processes online, and asking such questions as: What is the minimum number of participants needed to create an online group? Do group norms and cultures apply to Internet groups? Do groups tend to move to the extreme? Do online groups need leaders? Can I become an online leader? Who is the e-leader? What are the main hazards of e-leaders?

ARE GROUPS RELEVANT TO THE ONLINE EXPERIENCE?

What exactly do we mean when we talk about a group? The simple definition is three or more people that are dependent on each other, temporarily or constantly, in the pursuit of a common goal (Johnson & Johnson, 1994). So people walking along the street do not constitute a group, whereas people together on an organized bus tour in Tuscany do. In this section we will be considering different types of online group. We can divide them into three types: (1) those that are wholly online; (2) those whose main component is offline, but also have online elements, usually logistical; and (3) those whose main component is offline, but an online element has encroached and gradually become a leading component. We will be concentrating mainly on the first kind – groups that are wholly online – since this phenomenon has only been made possible by the Internet, and its growth and success are due to many of the Internet's components that we have been discussing throughout the book. Nevertheless, we will start by taking a look at the other two types of *partially online* group, and you will probably find that you are a member of at least one of them, possibly both, and that this has happened naturally, without you giving the matter much thought.

PARTIALLY ONLINE GROUPS

Today, it seems obvious to us all that when we belong to any sort of group – even if its essence is offline – it will have an online component, often a logistical one. For example, if you are a member of a book club that meets once a month, the dates for the meetings, the changes and cancellations, the refreshments, and so on, are organized online. In fact, today, the online component has become a seemingly essential part of any group activity. Even a one-off event like a wedding may well spawn a number of WhatsApp groups; for example, a chat group for close family members in different parts of the world might be shown photographs of the wedding dress. Many of us cannot imagine organizing any type of event without the aid of online tools.

The second type of partially online group is particularly fascinating. In this case, the group clearly started off as an offline group activity, for example a group of football supporters that meets up to go to matches, or a parenting course that meets once a week over a period of twelve weeks. Over time, contact between the members online gradually took on a life of its own, and the online component became equally important or, for some members, even more crucial. So, for example, the pre- and post-match analysis online became a vital part of the football team supporters' group, including a major component involving reporting and scrutiny for those unable to attend the game. As for the parenting group, as members tried out ideas they had encountered in the group meetings, and reported the results to other members online, the online component of the group grew. It became a way to make comparisons and introduce variations into the application of what they had learned, to collaborate on improvements, and further work together on what to discuss with the group leader. Thus, over time, the online part of the group became the focus, equal to or even surpassing the offline meetings. One of the reasons for this transfer from an offline to an online focus is that the advent and popularity of the portable device (the tablet or the smartphone) allows people to maintain contact with their group constantly, whereas the offline component is rigidly fixed in its allotted time space.

The third, and perhaps the most intriguing, types of group are those that exist exclusively online, that is, 100 percent of group activity happens online, and, unless something extreme happens, its members will never meet physically.

GROUPS THAT EXIST ONLY ONLINE

When I first started to conduct research in this field, people asked me: "Yair, you don't really believe you can find real social groups on the Internet, do you?" The prevailing attitude was that only geeks with no social life would form groups online to connect with other geeks. Specifically, a joke concerning the online fantasy community, Second Life, was doing the rounds: "Second life? Before you get a Second Life, try getting a real life first." The implication was that only lonely, anti-social, miserable individuals are members of online groups.

The Magnificent Seven factors described in Chapter 1 to account for the power of the Internet – Feeling of anonymity; Control over level of physical exposure; Control over communications; Ease in locating like-minded people; Accessibility and availability at all times and places; Feeling of equality; Fun of web surfing – explain very well the advantages of an online group. Just think about how anonymity helps people to enter groups which they would not dare to join in the offline world. Take, for example, an online group in Iran in which citizens voice criticism of their government; were its members to be identified, they would likely be put in prison or even sentenced to death. Another factor to consider is the control of physical exposure, the fact that the Internet allows people to control how they present themselves, reshaping their physical exposure as they wish. The power to control the online interaction allows people to join groups they would not join offline. They are likely to treat it as a kind of game, which they have the power to leave at any time they wish. The ease of finding a group of similar others means that you can find groups on any topic. When it comes to control, people feel in charge because they can carefully control their message in order to project the image that they choose. The fact that the Internet is available everywhere and all the time makes the online group likely to be more active than an offline group. And the factor of equality makes everyone feel comfortable. All together, we find ourselves easily and speedily members of a significant group, with no geographical constraints. Moreover, our group accompanies us everywhere, and provides us with role models, norms, and positive reinforcement.

Moving on, we will focus on groups whose activity is completely online, or at least a very dominant part of their existence.

CAN WE BE SIGNIFICANT INDIVIDUALS AND GROUP MEMBERS ON THE INTERNET SIMULTANEOUSLY?

If we return to the earlier task of completing five sentences starting with "I'm...," we will find that, although we define ourselves as group members, we are also likely to define ourselves as individuals. As human beings we strive to be both individuals and group members. Erich Fromm, the famous humanistic psychologist, suggested that we live our lives torn by the conflict that exists between fulfilling ourselves as individuals and belonging to a significant group that provides us with a group identity and a whole repertoire of group rewards (Fromm, 1941). The culture in which we live will help to decide on which side of the individuality/group balance we place the emphasis. Each choice, be it an emphasis on individuality or on group belonging, will involve both gains and losses. In an Eastern society, for example, the emphasis is on belonging to a group. However, while a person in such a society receives a significant group identity and group support, he is likely to find it difficult to fulfill himself as an individual. In many cases the group will determine for him what he should become professionally, whom he should marry, and how he should live. In a Western society that emphasizes individuality, a person is much more capable of fulfilling himself as an individual, but this is likely to be at the expense of identity with and belonging to a group. For example, in the Western world individuals are more likely to relocate due to a job opportunity. In many cases, this individual fulfillment will require them to leave the wider family behind.

I have suggested elsewhere that the Internet is a place where the conflict between individuality and belonging can be solved very effectively (Amichai-Hamburger, 2005a). In an offline setting, for many reasons, we are very limited regarding the types of group we can join. These reasons include logistics (Does the group exist and, if so, is it in my vicinity?); timing (Can I make meetings at that time?); and expense, transport, disabled access, and so on. In an online setting, the possibilities seem nearly endless. Just for fun, think of the most offbeat group you once dreamed of joining or may still want to. Now hunt for that kind of group using the main online search engines. Chances are, you'll find one. This is important, because it means that you can find a group that really fits your interests. This is likely to enhance the possibility that you'll be able to achieve the optimal combination of individual expression and feeling of belonging to a significant group. Online groups, which cover almost every possible existing hobby and interest, increase the likelihood of people finding a group that relates to their individual needs. Also, there is always the possibility that someone will initiate a new group that appeals to you. Being a member of a group that is constantly available and meets individual needs is one of the best guarantees that a human being will be able to resolve the tension between individuality and group belonging.

In addition, the online world tends to give us more power both over deciding to join a group and leaving it without social sanction or embarrassment. This is particularly likely in groups in which membership is anonymous, and is in stark contrast to the offline world, where exiting a group may involve hurting people's feelings and thus a sense of guilt. However, many young people today require confirmation from their group, for their most intimate individual experience. Thus blurring the divide between individuality and group belonging and damaging their individuality.

MINI-BIOGRAPHY: ERICH SELIGMANN FROMM

Erich Fromm (1900–1980) was a humanist psychologist. He was born to a traditional Jewish family in Frankfurt, and started his career as a psychoanalytical psychologist. He soon began to question what motivates people, and felt that the psychoanalytical explanation given by Freud was not satisfactory. He suggested that what motivates a person are higher human needs rather than basic animal ones. In his youth, he experienced World War I and the shocking suicide of a close family friend. Those difficult experiences left their mark on him and his attitude as a psychologist, challenging him to understand human psychological restraints.

When the National Socialist (Nazi) Party came to power in Germany in 1933, Fromm moved first to Geneva, Switzerland, and then to Columbia University, New York, and later to Mexico City University, Mexico.

In his classic book, *Escape from Freedom* (1941), Fromm wrote that, as a result of releasing himself from the chains of traditional society (for example, organized religion), man is seemingly capable of fulfilling his aspirations; however, this release from society's chains incurs the price of illusion and disappointment. In the modern world, people remain alienated and lonely and choose to solve the lack of meaning in their lives by connecting with strong, charismatic leaders who provide simple answers to complicated problems. According to Fromm, people should strive for uniqueness and real individuality. One of the most important components of his theory is the conflict between individuality and belonging.

WHAT IS THE MINIMUM CONDITION NEEDED TO CREATE A GROUP?

Over the years, social psychologists have attempted to understand what causes individuals to form themselves into groups. For a time, it was commonplace to assume that groups were created through a common destiny or as result of the interdependence of fate. In the 1970s, Henri Tajfel and his team at the University of Bristol challenged this assumption and demonstrated that even individuals who were divided into groups on a random basis, such as preferring the paintings of either Klee or Kandinsky, felt that they were part of a group (the Klee or Kandinsky fan club), and showed a preference for their own new group over the other group, even being prepared to donate more money to their own group (Taijfel et al., 1971).

In a study I conducted (Amichai-Hamburger, 2005b) before social networks had really taken off, I was interested to learn if people would feel part of an online group created on a random basis. At the time, it was not clear whether my results would reiterate those of Tajfel, because in my experiment there was an important difference – there was no physical proximity between the participants. This could mean that members would struggle to achieve a feeling of group affiliation. In the experiment, subjects who interacted with each other through the Internet were divided into two groups based on their preference for the work of either Klee or Kandinsky. They were then presented with two cognitive tasks whereby they were (1) shown a number of circles on a screen for a very brief period, and then asked to estimate, in groups, how many circles they had seen. This task was similar to that set by Tajfel. After reaching a decision within their own group, participants then (2) had to evaluate, individually, the accuracy of their group judgment in comparison to that of the other group. The results of this task indicated a clear group preference. As with Tajfel's experiment, each group's members thought that their group judgment was superior. It is important to note that the groups had been divided on a random basis. These results demonstrate that the Internet experience is very real and even a trivial allocation of people to a group is likely to create a strong sense of group identity. The speed with which we define ourselves as a member of a group, even when the main criteria for doing so is randomly assigned and the whole process is online, demonstrates the strong desire of people to belong. If group favoritism can be evoked so simply, consider what happens when real differences exist between groups, such as those based on religion, culture, and history of conflict.

IS ANONYMITY LIKELY TO ELIMINATE GROUP IDENTITY?

Initially, when anonymous online groups emerged, it was expected that offline group identity would be irrelevant; for example, an Irishman would not identify as such. In fact, people were found to behave according to the social identity model of deindividuation effects (the SIDE model) put forward by Lea, Spears, Watt, and Rogers (2000). This suggests that in a context in which group identity is salient, even though membership is anonymous, people will still behave according to their group identity. According to this theory, an individual has a complex self and it is the social environment that determines which aspect of one's identity will become active in a specific context. A group context is likely to affect people's thoughts and behavior according to their group identity, and they will thus behave according to group norms. In contrast, a context that focuses on the individual (that is, no group salience exists) will reduce the use of social categories. SIDE theory explains why group conflicts evident in the offline world may transfer to the online world, where people often behave according to group identities. Intergroup conflict is likely to occur when rival group members encounter each other online.

ARE GROUP NORMS AND CULTURES EVIDENT IN INTERNET GROUPS?

Norms are created within all groups. These norms are the behavioral codes that group members are expected to adhere to (Feldman, 1984). Group founders are generally very influential in establishing and defining the norms. As the group evolves, new norms are likely to be created and some of these are likely to replace original norms. A group is likely to adhere to formal and informal norms. Formal norms are those that the group identifies as the required official code of behavior from members. For example, not playing loud music late at night and disturbing the neighbors is a formal norm (in fact, in many countries "noise pollution" is a legal offense). Informal norms are not written but are nevertheless adhered to and expected of people; for example, table manners and polite forms of greeting (Ullmann, 1977).

We have all probably found ourselves in situations in which we are unsure of the formal or informal group norms, and, as a result, have had to study others carefully to learn how to behave. This situation is actually more likely to occur with informal norms. I was once invited to a formal dinner in England. Faced with an alarming array of cutlery, I had to continually peep to my left to see what item my more knowledgeable neighbor had picked.

Norms apply to online groups in a similar way. Every website contains a combination of formal and informal norms for surfers. In more democratic groups, there are processes in place for revision of these regulations; on such sites, group members can have a say in shaping group norms. In contrast, there are less democratic websites where the founders or administrators are completely in charge, at least of the formal norms. Between these two extremes, a whole range of possibilities exists.

Even on parts of the Internet where people are anonymous, which seemingly allows them to express themselves freely, there are still norms that define what is allowed, what is a gray area, and what is forbidden. Some members may eventually conform to the group norms by a process of trial and error as they test the boundaries, either intentionally or inadvertently, to see just how much flexibility there is, and what behavior will be punished. A user who does not obey a formal norm may well receive a punishment (although not all websites are designed to do this). For example, attempting to sell stolen goods on a commercial website is seen as a real offense, which breaks one of the basic formal norms. Doing so may well lead to a formal message and possibly a ban from the website; it may also result in the website reporting the offender to the authorities. When it comes to less formal norms the situation is more foggy. Suppose you were to visit a chatroom for the first time. The discussion is anonymous, and you make up a nickname. However, as a newcomer, you are wholly unaware that the nickname you have chosen is already used by another member. At first, you are likely to receive a comment from one of the regulars asking you to change your nickname. Should you decide to disregard this message, for example because you did not like its tone, you may well find that the other users shun you and ignore your contributions. This is an informal sanction, against a violation of an unofficial norm. Most participants will quickly pick up on what is expected of them, both in authorized and less-authorized ways.

Online groups may adhere to different norms – for example, a group member who is very popular in one group might find that the same set of behaviors lead to her acquiring a bad name or even censorship in a different group; sensitivity to specific norms and cultures for each group is thus important. Often, we are literally sitting in the same physical environment as we hop, in seconds, from one online group culture to another; thus, a special awareness may be required in order to move seamlessly between them.

CHATROOM: THE STORY OF SIMON

Simon is an old friend of mine who worked in high tech as a member of a virtual team. All members of this team were Israeli; most were located in Israel and some were located abroad. The workload was heavy and pressurized, and people were very open with one another on the team, conversing freely using whatever language came to mind. Simon reports, "We were often very rude to each other, but always with a smile."

After three years in that high tech company Simon moved on and found a new job, this time with a US company with an office in Israel. Simon was again chosen to work on a virtual team, this time with members from all around the globe but mostly Americans. Simon initially applied his virtual team member style when communicating with others in this new environment, but very quickly noticed that people were astonished and even appalled by his "frankness." Luckily, Simon was astute enough to get the message. He immediately dropped his casual, jocular confrontational communication style and quickly adapted to the more sensitive and polite style expected in this company. Simon succeeded in transforming himself efficiently and incurred no negative results. Unfortunately, not everyone can adapt so smoothly.

WHAT IS CONFORMITY AND HOW IS IT RELEVANT ONLINE?

Conformity is a social process that is likely to occur in every group, both traditional and online. When a group is establishing itself, the different opinions of individual members will surface, and the dominant opinion will ultimately emerge. Thereafter, many members will feel uncomfortable about expressing dissent with that dominant opinion for fear of experiencing embarrassment or shame and, as a result they will support it. In some cases it may even transpire that, in fact, the majority of group members dissented from the dominant opinion, but because no one wanted to be perceived as the deviant one, they all conformed to this unpopular view and it was ratified. As a result of conformity, groups may make a wrong decision and even a disastrous one.

The Japanese attack on Pearl Harbor during World War II provides a historical example of the disastrous results of conformity. Japanese aircraft surprised the US army and inflicted heavy losses: 8 battleships were damaged, 188 aircraft were destroyed, and 2,403 Americans were killed. The US army was, at the time, following every move of the Japanese army; however, the dominant opinion among US decision makers was that the Japanese were not actually going to launch an attack on US territory. There were some who thought differently, but no one had the courage speak up, and so no preparations were made for such an attack, never mind a preemptive strike.

The "line experiment" conducted by Solomon Asch (1951) is the most famous means of studying conformity. In this experiment, groups of seven participants were told that they were to take part in a vision test; more specifically, they were to evaluate the comparative length of a line drawn on a piece of paper. In fact each group contained only one genuine participant, the other members where cooperating with the experimenter. The group was presented with a line and asked to choose and state aloud which out of another three lines (A, B, or C) was of an identical length. When tested individually people had no problem picking out the right line. In the group situation it was arranged that the genuine subject would announce their decision last. One after another the confederate group members pointed at a wrong line. This placed the genuine participant in a quandary: whether to conform with the group norm or go with what they knew to be the right answer. Asch carried out 18 trials, and found that 75 percent of participants conformed at least once.

In a similar manipulation, but carried out online (Rosander & Eriksson, 2012), 52.6 percent of participants pointed at least once to the wrong line. The results of this experiment suggest that conformity is as relevant online as it is offline.

MINI-BIOGRAPHY: SOLOMON ELIOT ASCH

Solomon Asch (1907–1996) was a US pioneer in the field of social psychology. Born in Poland, at the age of thirteen Asch emigrated with his family to the United States. His childhood in the Lower East Side was challenging and he also found learning English very difficult. Despite his initial difficulties, Asch went on to become a gestalt psychologist; that is, he was very interested in perception – specifically, how a person creates a whole impression from little bits of information – in fact, he contributed significantly to the field of impression formation. His most famous experiments were conducted in the field of conformity. Interestingly, Asch told his colleagues that his idea to study conformity was brought about by his childhood experiences in Poland. He recalled being seven years old and staying up for his first Passover seder, the Jewish ceremonial meal recalling the Exodus from Egypt. As is the custom, an extra glass of wine was poured and left in the middle of the table. When the young Asch asked who it was for, he was told it was for the prophet Elijah, who, according to custom, would arrive indiscernibly, at the appropriate time in the ritual, and drink from the cup. His uncle assured him that if he watched very carefully he would see the wine move as a sip was taken from it. Asch remembered being filled with a sense of suggestion and expectation, and with the encouragement of all the adults around him, [thinking] he saw the level of wine in the cup drop just a bit. Thus, early in life, he succumbed to the pressure to conform, which, he believes, fostered his idea to investigate conformity later in life.

DO ONLINE GROUPS TEND TO MOVE TO EXTREME POSITIONS?

All groups have a tendency to move toward an extreme position, particularly when the group's members share the values on which the group was built (Myers & Lamm, 1975). As stated earlier, individuals wish to be members of a significant group and also have a need for individual expression. This dichotomy of needs is likely to cause individual members to express more extreme opinions in comparison to other group members, in an effort to assert their own individuality. As each group member shares this same need, it is very likely that, as time moves on, the group will become increasingly extreme in its views. This process can be observed in many online groups. For example, a member of an online environmental group that is currently engaged in building wider public support for the preservation of a row of trees slated for removal when a new road is built may well, during a group discussion, express more extreme opinions about the aims of the campaign than those originally held. As more group members move in this direction, the entire group will express increasingly extreme opinions. This is very likely to affect the actions taken in the name of their cause.

CHATROOM: NIKI, THE SOCIAL ACTIVIST

Niki lives in New York, where she is studying for an MA in Social Psychology at Brooklyn College. She lives close to the campus with two of her friends and is very involved in social activities there. She is a gentle person, very warm and sensitive to others; last year she adopted two homeless dogs. Niki and her family have always been active members of the Democratic Party. A few months ago, she joined a Facebook group supporting state-funded abortion. Gradually she noticed that the group was becoming increasingly extreme in its views. Discussions that had started respectfully were becoming more militant in their attitude to anti-abortion campaign leaders, even to the point of suggesting taking violent action against them. Niki also noticed that she, too, was adopting more extreme views in parallel with those of the group, and that in order to be heard and to receive feedback, she had to take up ever more extreme positions. Niki did not like the impact the group was having on her and decided to leave.

DO ONLINE GROUP MEMBERS GIVE THEIR BEST EFFORTS?

To be successful, groups sometimes depend on maximizing each individual's efforts to achieve group goals. Should individual members not give their best, the group will fail to fulfill its potential. This failure by individual members to put forward their maximum effort frequently arises from their perception that their lack of effort will be sufficiently masked by the efforts of others. As more group members arrive at the same conclusion, group productivity is likely to diminish. This phenomenon is called social loafing (Latané, Williams, & Harkins, 1979; Steiner, 1972). We see this phenomenon in many online groups, particularly those aiming to achieve a goal, be it a formal task for a group of employees (in a global high tech company, for example) or a voluntary task (fundraising on the part of a charity committee, for example). However, it is much more likely to occur in online groups where membership is voluntary, especially in groups lacking a clear mission, goals, and objectives. The fact that many members may lack a deep commitment to group goals makes this situation even more predictable. Moreover, on the Internet, when people are not identifiable, this phenomena is likely to be even more prevalent.

Several solutions to social loafing have been suggested, and these can also apply to online groups (Amichai-Hamburger, Koslowsky, & Beckenstein-Aviran, 2000). Here is a breakdown of the eight solutions that can help curtail social loafing:

1. *Purpose* – the group should have a clear purpose. Why is the endeavor worthwhile?
2. *Goals* – the group should have a clear statement of what it is aiming to accomplish.
3. *Objectives* – the group should provide clear descriptions of exactly what is to be done.
4. *Personal importance* – the purpose of the group has to be relevant to all group members.
5. *Challenging tasks* – the group's objectives need to be translated into interesting and challenging tasks.
6. *Dependency* – each group member must feel that the group depends on their individual investment of motivation and effort.
7. *Individual tasks* – group members need to be able to see that their individual efforts are measured and that they will receive feedback on them. Being personally responsible for actions will cause them to work harder. For this reason, the number of individual obligations within the group should be maximized.

When applying these solutions to online groups aiming to achieve defined goals, a strong dependency between rights and obligations needs to exist. People must create a dependency between their rights as group members and the obligations the group is asking them to uphold. Successful groups create a mechanism whereby individual members can obtain more rights as they take on more obligations that help the group to achieve its goals. This applies especially to online voluntary groups, since in a formal task group the connection between rights and obligations is clearer. In voluntary groups, we have to put a greater emphasis on the emotional attachment of the workers to the group purpose. The emotional bonding of group members and commitment to group goals stimulate the involvement of individuals. As individual group members feel more committed to a goal, and more part of a cohesive group, they are likely to work harder. If you add to it a measurable task for each group member, this is likely to guarantee that each group member will produce their best efforts and so minimize the phenomenon of social loafing. It is amazing how much a group can achieve when all members are giving it their best effort.

CHATROOM: PREVENTING SOCIAL LOAFING IN TEAMS

At the university where I teach, I am running a project with my students, for which they have divided themselves into teams of five. The task assigned to each team is to initiate, build, and market a website that helps a particular disadvantaged group in the global village. When I converse with the students, I make a conscious effort to utilize all eight solutions to social loafing. For example, I emphasize the ethical importance of the project; I focus on goals and the significance of individual contributions; I make sure that each group has a substantial challenge to work on. Since the students need to learn about effective team-building, I teach them the principles of how they can prevent social loafing within the team. I urge them to see the project as a jigsaw puzzle, the resolution of which involves utilizing all human resources in their team – in other words, I help them appreciate all the different abilities and talents within their group, and to understand how they will be required to complete the task. They have to make sure that each team member has a specific responsibility, so that each person feels that they own a specific piece of the puzzle, and has an obligation to deliver it within the agreed upon time-span so that the whole puzzle will be completed on schedule. This group work division creates a strong individual dependency whereby members feel that they depend on one another to complete the task. All together, they create a strong team identity, which creates a high degree of cohesiveness. I have very high expectations for the success of this project.

DO WE NEED LEADERS ONLINE?

In general, groups benefit from having leaders who help members achieve their goals; this is particularly true when the goals are complex and it is necessary to have an authority figure to coordinate the group. However, scholars have long understood that some of the reasons purporting to explain why we feel we need leaders are irrational (Hamburger, 2000). One of the less rational reasons is what we might call *simplification*: leaders simplify our world into something we can understand. The leader provides us with simple explanations for problematic and complicated issues. Traditional history books focus on leaders as the main, and sometimes the only, explanation for historical events, ignoring the complexity of the socio-economic variables involved. Leaders themselves provide us with simple explanation for very complicated situations.

Another irrational explanation for why we need leaders is *projection*. This theory suggests that our leader provides a form of compensation for the loss of the total power we felt in our very early infant lives. According to this psychoanalytic school of thought, when a child is born, she cannot differentiate between herself and the environment. When she cries, she receives nourishment or is held; thus she develops the perception that her mother exists for the sole purpose of providing for her wants, and by extension, that the world exists to answer her needs. Gradually and slowly, she realizes that her needs are not always provided for immediately; she learns painfully that her mother and the entire environment are separate from her and do not exist for the sole reason of satisfying her needs. A certain kind of leader can compensate for the painful feelings generated by this traumatic loss of power that, even as we leave childhood to become adults, are always a part of us. Relating to the leader answers our most narcissistic needs, allowing us to imagine that we are once again the center of the world.

Transference is another irrational reason for the desire for a leader. This theory states that the leader is a replacement for the loss of the super-competent figure played by our early childhood caregivers, usually a father or mother, who protected us from the world's dangers. Slowly and gradually, we realize that our parents are not super-heroes, that they have faults and cannot provide total protection for us. This knowledge leaves us feeling very vulnerable in a frightening world. By connecting to a leader, we achieve a subconscious replacement of our parent. The super-competent figure of our childhood is replaced, in the shape of a leader who will protect us.

The final irrational explanation is *meaning*. It suggests that people strive for meaning, and without it, feel that their lives are merely a meaningless and random encounter of stimuli. Leaders can provide followers with a purpose for their existence. This can be the case with leaders who fight for the rights of the poor and the weak, but it can also apply to those leaders who inspire their followers with racist theories and rhetoric, promising them that they will control the future world.

It seems, then, that people have both conscious and unconscious reasons for desiring leadership. As our world moves increasingly online, these same reasons play a significant role in our need for online leadership.

CAN ANYONE BECOME AN ONLINE LEADER?

This is a very interesting question, one that may be addressed by refer-
ring to a traditional leadership theory. Great man theory argues that
some people are born with unique traits that prepare them to become
leaders in any situation. According to this theory, someone born a
leader will always be a leader, while those born without such genetic
traits will never become leaders. This theory was widely accepted until
the nineteenth century and used to justify the differences in status
between royals and the common people. In the past, being born into
a royal or aristocratic family defined you as having "blue blood," that
is, being genetically equipped for a leadership role. In keeping with
this theory, one should assume that all major leaders possess an identical list of traits. However, no such list actually exists. Consider Moses,
Mahatma Gandhi, Winston Churchill, and Martin Luther King Jr. Do
they possess identical traits? Of course not; they are different from
each other in many respects. Certainly, some common traits exist, but
very few that we could consider obligatory for leadership. This has led
to the development of new leadership theories, one of which is situational leadership theory. According to this idea, the leader emerges
not as a result of genetic traits, but rather is someone who is in the
right place at the right time. This person relies on their followers and
the situation to maintain their leadership position.

Interestingly, throughout the world, royal families (that is, those who
were granted their position in accordance with the great man theory)
are currently using the Internet to justify and bolster their super-status
among their followers. This is taken to the extreme in certain areas,
where members of the royal family are using the Internet to deliver
their message, rationalizing their total power in an attempt to brain-
wash their subjects. They utilize different media channels, including
the Internet, in their efforts to create total identification between the
people and the rulers. In general, a royal family's official website will
market its legitimacy through time, claiming that its power is God-
given. Thus, any dissent from this viewpoint or action taken against
the royals is, in fact, directed against the people themselves. (Never
mind the fact that, in totalitarian countries, the Internet can be monitored as a means of crushing dissent or competition for the leadership
role, thus transforming it from a channel of freedom of speech to one
that serves the anti-democratic regime.)

Situational leadership theory argues that anyone can become a leader if their qualities fit the context, and thus leaders come and go; if they don't adapt effectively to new situations, they don't hold on to power. One modern example of this theory is provided in the form of formal working task groups in global organizations. Such organizations have to create online groups of people from different locations in the world; members could thus be working in places as diverse as London, Shanghai, Calcutta, and New York. Since the membership is very diverse, the leadership role tends to be flexible, and is dependent on the topic being discussed.

As we discussed in earlier chapters, research on personality and online behavior found that, on the Internet, nobody knows if you are an introvert, and so people with social inhibitions are likely to feel protected and empowered in that environment (Hamburger & Ben-Artzi, 2000). When they feel protected, introverts are more likely to express themselves freely when online, and it could even be assumed that such individuals might feel comfortable enough to assume leadership roles, perhaps for the first time in their lives.

You can also witness situational leadership coming to the fore in the amazing dynamics of social movements and protest on the Internet. People who come with a real will to do good create Internet groups to effect genuine social and political change around the world. In their offline lives, some of these people would not necessarily be leaders, but the Internet has helped them to find their voices.

IS CHARISMA RELEVANT TO BEING A LEADER IN THE ONLINE WORLD?

Another popular leadership theory is that of the transformational leader. It is called transformational because it rejects the assumption that a leader is dependent on their situation and followers, but rather has the power to transform the context and not to be subject to it. Such a leader has the power to create a new set of perceptions among followers by making them focus on their higher needs and not their individual interests, thus creating a positive future picture which followers will want to be part of. This in turn encourages such followers to make efforts far greater than they previously believed themselves capable of.

Transformational leadership is premised on four primary traits: charisma, inspirational motivation, intellectual stimulation, and individualized consideration (Burns, 1978). *Charisma* is the degree to which leadership behavior produces admiration, identification, and respect. This is mainly achieved by the leader's willingness to take risks and follow a core set of values. *Inspirational motivation* refers to the leader's success in making their vision relevant and appealing. This demands superb communication skills. *Intellectual stimulation* is the ability of the leader to make followers challenge their perceptions of their own abilities and potential. This is achieved mainly by involving followers in the decision-making process and stimulating their efforts to be creative and innovative in fulfilling their duties and completing their tasks. *Individualized consideration* refers to a leader's ability to create the feeling among followers that he cares about them and their needs. Here, the challenge is to identify those individual needs and make the larger leadership vision relevant to them.

The Internet constitutes a unique and amazing environment for transformational leadership, because here the leader can inspire millions of people throughout the world. Transformational leadership is thus especially relevant in the Internet era, and can illuminate the nature of leadership online, that is, e-leadership.

HOW CAN ONE BECOME AN E-LEADER?

To start I would like to suggest that we all have the potential to become an e-leader. Even those of us who do not see ourselves as leaders may come across a topic, say in an article about a social issue, and become fired up. Since on the Internet no one cares that you have no leadership experience, you can utilize the potential of the Internet to further your cause.

Becoming an e-leader is easier than you think. There are ten basic guidelines that can help anyone become an online leader. Let's break them down.

DIGITAL LITERACY

This is the ability to use online channels to build and promote your leadership (Eshet-Alkalai, 2004). To be an online leader, you must learn how to use the Internet to transfer your message. For example,

YouTube can help you to translate your vision and messages into a visual clip (helpful tip: keep it short). Or, you can use Facebook to create a group of supporters and give them the ability to get involved. Twitter is good for short real-time messages that give the followers the feeling that they are part of your life. If done properly, online messages can create a sense of intimacy between you and your followers. Remember, you as the leader do not have to do everything yourself; however, the messages you send are far more effective if they are all in your name. If a follower discovers that the message he received from the leader via Twitter a second ago – which created a feeling of intimacy between them – was actually crafted and sent by a media expert, the leader's image will probably be tarnished. It is also important to be aware that, as your Facebook group grows in size, maintaining a personal touch and feeling of intimacy with its members will become increasingly challenging. In today's Web2 era, people want to feel that they are an active part of a movement, not merely passive players. In order to do this and really get them involved, it is necessary to acknowledge their written contributions on Facebook, no matter how numerous.

BUILD TRUST

This is the basis for a strong, positive relationship between leader and followers (Dirks & Ferrin, 2002). Much of your leadership credibility will be determined based on whether you keep your promises. Promising but not delivering will reduce your legitimacy as a leader. Bear in mind that the virtual world does not justify virtual promises; in that sense, it is a real world with a need to keep real promises. Take, for example, offering to support a project via an online volunteering website. Some people might think that not honoring this commitment is not a problem because it was a "virtual promise." However, that decision has real-life consequences for the people relying on that particular project. Leaders have to realize that, in this regard, online and offline are the same.

OPEN COMMUNICATION

In the online world people expect a leader to address them as equals. Open communication will encourage people to get involved (Barge, 2003). This is particularly important in a virtual business organization;

managers who address only business matters – as opposed to including elements of personal communication – fail to understand that the Internet is a tool for promoting real interaction with real people. Making people feel a personal connection to the organization is the best way to get them involved and to maximize their potential. Their involvement is likely to lead to a greater commitment and an increase in productivity. Open communication can be encouraged through the personal touch, something as simple as sending a worker an e-birthday card.

ACCESS TO INFORMATION

In all organizations some people will naturally be closer to the leader than others, and thus have greater access to information (Mayfield & Mayfield, 2002). This situation can very easily become an obstacle in the group process, since a sense of inequality can affect people's actions. In the digital global world we live in, people demand equality with others. Therefore, open access to all task-related information is an absolute must. Workers or participants will understand that some information, for reasons of security, is unavailable to them, but if they are denied access to information based only on their lower status, this will affect their commitment to the organization. We have to bear in mind that often team members are located in places physically remote from central leadership, and may even be representing your company within another organization. Open communication with their mother organization is a vital factor in making them feel part of the organization. If done properly, it renders geographical distances irrelevant.

TASK ORIENTATION

Many online groups are trying to achieve important, worthwhile goals. However, sometimes they are either not clear about their goals or their members are not motivated by them. With the cooperation of group members, leaders need to clarify group goals and establish a clear process for achieving them. The first step is getting group members to realize that, to achieve best results, they have to get involved and, at least metaphorically, get their hands dirty. In voluntary online groups, it is necessary to identify those people who seem to be more active, and request that they lead mini, subtasks and involve people from the secondary, less-involved circle of group members. As we learned earlier from research into social loafing, the main principle is to try to give each of these group members a specific task that can be measured, so it is possible to provide them with feedback. We must remain mindful that we are dealing with volunteers, and therefore have to continually stress the vision we are all working toward, so as to guarantee that, while we focus on the work, we don't lose their emotional involvement. This involvement is based on goodwill; in many cases, after the initial wave of enthusiasm, if the group does not translate its vision into a program of significant action, the group is likely to disappear. In formal groups, there are usually set procedures in place and people tend to produce results. Even then, we need to understand that, in many cases, even these achievements are likely to be way below the real potential of the group, due to some or even many group members not doing their best. Therefore our role as leaders is to work towards getting them to identify with the vision and commit to working hard to fulfill it.

EMOTIONAL FOCUS

Western culture used to put great emphasis on cognitive intelligence (IQ), that is, the ability to think and reason. IQ was considered to be the most accurate predictor of success in life. Today, we know that our emotional indigence (EQ), that is, the ability to understand and manage our emotions and the emotions of others, is at least as important, if not more so (Houpt Gilkey & Ehringhaus, 2015). Emotional emphasis is closely linked to the skill set of the transformational leader. The greater the capacity of a leader to read others' emotions and transfer them successfully, the stronger the impact they are likely to have on the emotional world of their followers, which directly affects the strength of that leader's impact. An online leader needs to be able to deliver a message to which followers can respond on an emotional level. The content needs to be such that followers feel that they are part of something bigger than their own day-to-day lives. Thus, the message will aim to induce the group member to relate to the vision emotionally, whilst simultaneously expressing an understanding of and concern for the challenges faced by the individual follower in their daily life. It is about relating to the emotions people express, articulating excitement, and optimism in fulfilling the vision. Obama did just that in his successful 2008 campaign message, "Yes We Can." The best message is one that unites the emotions of the individual with the vision of the group. The emotional link prompts the followers to perceive their leader as fulfilling an unconscious need, such as providing a simplification of the complex world, compensating them for their early childhood traumas, and providing significant meaning in life.

CHALLENGE THE PARADIGMS OF FOLLOWERS

The leader has to help followers redefine their "ability paradigm," that is, their beliefs regarding what they can do and achieve. This is an essential part of transformational leadership in the offline world, and is an equally important factor in online leadership. It is quite natural that each group member has a strong idea of their own capabilities (and what they're not capable of). This perception, while seemingly objective, is actually completely subjective. To provide a psychological explanation: assumptions about our abilities are often the result of expectations planted in our self-perception by early caregivers such as parents. Such ideas about ourselves can often work as a self-fulfilling prophecy, whereby we (subconsciously) set ourselves up to fail when we try to push past the limits we grew up seeing in ourselves. The leader must challenge those paradigms by encouraging followers to confront their own limitations and recognize that they are subjective rather than objective. Next, the leader needs to prove their point by creating a gradual sequence of tasks for followers to complete, starting with small challenges and gradually moving towards more demanding activities. Self-efficacy theory (Bandura, 1977) specifies that the first task should be a gentle challenge of the paradigm, enhancing the likelihood that group members will experience success; from there, in a gradual process, the leader will slowly increase the challenge. In this way, group members will build their sense of self-efficacy and, perhaps most importantly, their belief in their own abilities (ibid.). Online leadership requires that the leader follows and encourages group members' progress. In volunteer online groups, the reward will be more psychological; in a formal task group, it will be psychological as well as financial.

VISION

This is an inseparable component of transformational leadership both offline and online. The vision is a positive picture of a future world; it is a road map, with a starting point (where we are) and a powerful focus on the destination (our goal). The transformational leader promises followers that they will be led to a bright future if they follow his message. Imagine an organization of 30,000 people, spread over 8 countries and 74 different locations. Despite the huge geographical constraints, one click of the keyboard is all it takes for each worker to receive a message from the leader, focusing on the vision and written in a way that speaks to him or her individually. In this way, with the right formula, anyone can take on an online global leadership role.

ESTABLISHING A CULTURE THROUGH THE NET

The concept of culture includes the meaningful beliefs and values that the group shares. Leaders strive to influence the behavior of group members through the creation of a group culture which is consistent with their values. Newcomers to the group will quickly learn the dominant cultural values and will adapt their perception and behavior accordingly (Schein, 1985). The main tools the leader uses to create group culture are symbols, stories, jargon, and ceremonies, as described below:

- *Symbols* are a means of conveying an organization or website's culture. They can encapsulate a set of common norms, a language, and commonalities between members (Louis, 1983). For example, should you start a new job in an office, you are likely to learn about the organizational culture from the physical environment around you. A common dominant feature is the organizational logo. Consider Apple's logo: a deeply bitten apple can be understood as representing both desire and knowledge. Every organization is trying to convey messages through its use of symbols; the challenge facing the online leader is how to move the power of such symbols into the realm of the Internet. Such leaders think of their websites as physical organizations, where it is vital that people visiting will immediately understand the organizational symbols, and what they portray. These symbols represent the values of an organization or website – the family, creativity, or high quality goods with no compromises, for example.

- *Stories* are a powerful tool for transmitting organizational values. When the stories distributed among a group are consistent with the leader's values, group culture is likely to be positively affected. A good story is worth a great deal and the Internet provides many channels through which to spread it. If the purpose of your online organization is to encourage young people to volunteer for overseas development projects, you need to post stories about happy volunteers, the difference they have made in the lives of others, and the sense of personal satisfaction they gained. However, if your stories do not ring true because they contradict the actual values of the organization, they will fail to have a positive impact.
- *Jargon* is an effective way to make members of an online organization feel part of a specific culture. Only those in the know will understand the key words, concepts, and metaphors used by your organization, which will give them a sense of belonging..
- *Ceremonies* are used by physical organizations as opportunities to bring staff together, and for leaders to reinforce organizational values and celebrate the successes of the organization. Online, leaders can utilize this concept to their advantage in that ceremonies are easy to document and to replay continually for their followers. Say, for example, that your organization values creativity. You could create an online competition challenging followers to be creative, with a serious incentive as a prize. This could be followed by an online prize-giving ceremony promoting the creativity of the winner and, by default, your organization. This concept could be taken one step further: each week the organization could set a different creative challenge. If the leader declares that winning ideas will affect group processes, this too is likely to encourage people to join in, watch the ceremonies, and participate actively in such events. In this way, ceremonies are likely to affect group culture.

Overall, there are a variety of promising tools that e-leaders can use to develop a shared culture via the Internet.

CREATIVITY

Creativity is the very soul of e-leadership (Sosik Kahai & Avolio, 1998). In the digital world, change is the only constant. You must be open to change and able to challenge the paradigms both you and other people associate with your organization. New technologies create new opportunities to do just that. In order to enhance creativity in an organization, leaders can introduce mechanisms for generating new ideas into the group process, such as brain-storming sessions. Such sessions also play an important role in promoting feelings of involvement and responsibility among group members. Only by enhancing creativity to its maximum is the group likely to fulfill its potential. Reaching such a level is very rewarding and contributes significantly to group dynamics and the ability of the group to achieve its goals.

In short, these "ten commandments" are tools for success in online leaders; by adopting them, anyone can become an online transformational leader. The core of the group is its task and the emotional emphasis of the participants. By working carefully and creating a win–win perspective among members, the leader is likely to produce a real group synergy, where the joint results are far greater than the sum of individual abilities.

WHAT ARE THE MAIN HAZARDS FACING E-LEADERS?

Each online leader is their own biggest challenge. A leader who has experienced success is likely to become passive and stop being creative. There are also hazards within the open communication system with the group's members, as this can easily become something that looks like open communication but is in fact one-sided, delivered by the leader to followers, with little real interaction. Another challenge for leaders is maintaining effective and measured communication. Bombarding followers with an overflow of information is counterproductive. Communication needs to be focused on two important goals: the task at hand and the strengthening of emotional bonding. When there is too much information, followers cannot absorb the messages, and they may stop reading them altogether. This will negatively impact followers' perceptions of their leader. The Internet gives leaders the power to share information with followers to get them more involved, but it entails the risk that the exercise can become an ego trip. One related aspect is the temptation of the leader to spy on their group members. This is more likely to happen in formal working groups, and can very easily cause the leader to be ousted from their position, and may even lead to the closure of the group.

A FINAL WORD

It seems incredible that, just a few years ago, people were convinced that online groups weren't really groups, but merely catered to geeks who had no life outside of the Internet. Today, online groups are an undeniable reality. For the first time in history, we have groups accompanying us wherever we go. Our groups are active, all around us, all day. This is very can be very empowering. However, it is important to stress that, while groups and their leaders are certainly significantly empowered by the net, the direction they choose to take may be positive or negative. It is also extremely important to stress that, in our digital age, anyone can become a leader. Groups come and go: leadership is the key factor in groups achieving their aims. A word of warning, when a charismatic leader succeeds in creating a cohesive online group which supports him, the groups is likely to ignore any outside information and deteriorate into a stage of post-truth, where the leader is only source of truth, (or otherwise).

REFERENCES

Amichai-Hamburger, Y. (2005a). Personality and the Internet. In Y. Amichai-Hamburger (Ed.), *The Social Net: Human Behavior in Cyberspace* (pp. 27–55). New York: Oxford University Press.

Amichai-Hamburger, Y. (2005b). Internet minimal group paradigm. *CyberPsychology and Behavior*, 8, 140–142.

Amichai-Hamburger, Y., Koslowsky, M., & Beckenstein-Aviran, D. (2000). The construction of the social loafing questionnaire. In M. Koslowsky & S. Stashevsky (Eds.), *Work Values and Organizational Behavior: Toward the New*

Millennium. Proceedings of the Seventh Bi-Annual Conference of the International Society for the Study of Work and Organizational Values (ISSWOV), pp. 211–216). Jerusalem: ISAS International Seminars.

Arrow, H., McGrath, J. E., & Berdahl, J. L. (2000). *Small Groups as Complex Systems: Formation, Coordination, Development and Adaptation.* Thousand Oaks, CA: Sage.

Asch, S. (1951). Effects of group pressure upon the modification and distortion of judgment. In H. Guetzkow (Ed.), *Groups, Leadership, and Men*. Pittsburgh, PA: Carnegie.

Bandura, A. (1977). Self-efficacy: Toward a unifying theory of behavioral change. *Psychological Review*, 84, 191–215.

Barge, J. K. (1994). *Leadership: Communication Skills for Organizations and Groups*. New York: St. Martin's Press.

Barge, J. K. (2003). Hope, communication, and community building. *Southern Communication Journal*, 69, 63–81.

Dirks, K. T., & Ferrin, D. L. (2002). Trust in leadership: Meta-analytic findings and implications for research and practice. *Journal of Applied Psychology*, 87, 611–628.

Dvir, T., Eden, D., Avolio, B., & Shamir, B. (2002). Impact of transformational leadership on follower development and performance: A field experiment. *Academy of Management Journal*, 45, 735–744.

Eshet-Alkalai, Y. (2004). Digital literacy: A conceptual framework for survival skills in the digital era. *Journal of Educational Multimedia and Hypermedia*, 13, 93–106.

Feldman, D. C. 1984. The development and enforcement of group norms. *Academy of Management Review*, 9, 47–53.

Fromm, E. (1941). *Escape from Freedom*. New York: Rinehart.

Fromm, E. (1973). *The Anatomy of Human Destructiveness*. New York: Henry Holt.

Goleman, D. (1995). *Emotional Intelligence*. New York: Bantam Books.

Hamburger, Y. (2000). Mathematical leadership vision. *Journal of Psychology*, 134, 601–611.

Houpt, J. L., Gilkey, R. L., & Ehringhaus, S. H. (2015). *Learning to Lead in the Academic Medical Center: A Practical Guide*. New York: Springer.

Johnson, D., & Johnson, R. (1994). *Learning Together and Alone: Cooperative, Competitive, and Individualistic Learning*. Needham Heights, MA: Prentice Hall.

Latané, B., Williams, K., & Harkins, S. (1979). Many hands make light the work: The causes and consequences of social loafing. *Journal of Personality and Social Psychology*, 37, 822–832.

Lea, M., Spears, R., Watt, S. E., & Rogers, P. (2000). The InSIDE story: Social psychological processes affecting on-line groups. In T. Postmes, M. Lea, R. Spears, & S. D. Reicher (Eds.), *SIDE Issues Centre Stage: Recent Developments in Studies of De-individuation in Groups* (pp. 47–62). Amsterdam: KNAW.

Lenham, R. (1995). Digital literacy. *Scientific American*, 273, 253–255.

Louis, M. R. (1983). Organizations as culture-bearing milieu. In L. W. Pondy, P. J. Frost, G. Morgan, & T. C. Dandridge (Eds.), *Organizational Symbolism* (pp. 39–54). Greenwich, CT: JAI Press.

Mayer, J. D., & Salovey, P. (1997). What is emotional intelligence? In P. Salovey & D. Sluyter (Eds.), *Emotional Development and Emotional Intelligence: Implications for Educators* (pp. 3–31). New York: Basic Books.

Mayfield, J., & Mayfield, M. (2002). Leader communication strategies: Critical paths to improving employee commitment. *American Business Review*, 20, 89–94.

Myers, D. G., & Lamm, H. (1975). The polarizing effect of group discussion. *American Scientist*, 63, 297–303.

Rosander, M., & Eriksson, O. (2012). Conformity on the Internet The role of task difficulty and gender differences. *Computers in Human Behavior*, 28, 1587–1595.

Schein, E. H. (1985). *Organizational Culture and Leadership*. San Francisco, CA: Jossey-Bass.

Smilowitz, M., Compton, C. D., & Flint, L. (1988). The effect of computer mediated communication on an individual's judgement: A study based on the methods of Asch's social influence experiment. *Computers in Human Behavior*, 4, 311–321.

Smircich, L. (1983). Organizations as shared meanings. In L. W. Pondy, P. J. Frost, G. Morgan, & T. C. Dandridge (Eds.), *Organizational Symbolism* (pp. 55–65). Greenwich, CT: JAI Press.

Sosik, J. J., Kahai, S. S., & Avolio, B. J. (1998). Transformational leadership and dimensions of creativity: Motivating idea generation in computer-mediated groups. *Creativity Research Journal*, 11, 111–122.

Tajfel, H., Billig, M. G., Bundy, R. P., & Flament, C. (1971). Social categorisation and intergroup behaviour. *European Journal of Social Psychology*, 1, 149–178.

Ullmann, M. E. (1977). *The Emergence of Norms*. Oxford: Oxford University Press.

7

HOW CAN WE USE THE INTERNET TO CREATE A BETTER WORLD?

There are people in this world who want to do good in their lives.... The online volunteering organization is a great place to serve humanity and experience self-satisfaction, even pleasure.

– online volunteer

Throughout this book, we have stressed that the empowerment we experience online can be used both positively and negatively. In this chapter, happily, we will be discussing a positive form of empowerment – using the Internet for prosocial activity that can really change the world!

Prosocial behavior is defined as a voluntary act toward another without the expectation of an immediate reward (Spacapan & Oskamp, 1992). It is an altruistic act. Alfred Adler, one of the founders of humanistic psychology theory, believed that humans have a real, true, and pure desire to do good in the world. Based on his teachings and that of others, we can understand the power of people to do good on the Internet.

MINI-BIOGRAPHY: ALFRED ADLER

Alfred Adler (1870–1937) was born to a Jewish family in Vienna. He was so ill as a child that doctors didn't believe that he would live. However, Adler went on to thrive. He worked in the field of psychology, becoming a core member of the esteemed Vienna Psychoanalytic Society (together with Sigmund Freud) and even serving as its president. However, when his own ideas started to be seen as too radical, he was ejected from the society. His ideas, which became known as Adlerian psychology, strongly advocated that every human being has the power to avoid becoming a slave to their past. Perhaps informed by the inferiority complex he experienced as a child, Adler stressed that people can become change agents in their own lives. In stark contrast to the Freudian idea that everything stems from our "id," namely, our animal instincts, he posited that a person is born with pure, positive powers which he defined as the ego. Conversely, according to Freudian theory, the ego merely regulates between the pressures of the id and the superego, the societal moral values we have assimilated. Later on, he added to his theory the need for self-actualization, and he specified social involvement as an essential factor in human well-being. Adler became one of the leaders of the humanistic psychology movement that understands people as moral beings and seekers after meaning.

Freud did not approve of Adler's independent thinking and disparaged him, calling him a dwarf. Adler's reply has become a part of the pantheon of psychological statements. As legend has it, he replied: "The dwarf on the shoulders of the giant can see farther than the giant."

In this chapter we will be considering a series of compelling questions, such as: Can we use the Internet to improve the world? What are the special advantages of online volunteering? We'll be reading accounts from an inspiring cross-section of volunteers, and will also be discussing the challenges and rewards of projects that exist to promote contact between rival groups. Can the Internet support such intergroup contact? When intergroup contact takes place in uncontrolled and unsupervised virtual spaces, what is likely to be the result? Can games help to improve intergroup relationships? What additional ideas can we use to counter stereotypes and improve intergroup relationships?

Countless projects designed to create significant prosocial change around the world exist on the Internet. Examples of such projects are those which promote the empowerment of women, discussion groups on alternative energy solutions in Africa, and websites to teach kids math. These projects are usually above and beyond the abilities of a single individual and are run in cooperation with other people.

One of my favorite examples is Guerrilla Gardening (Amichai-hamburger, 2006), which reminds me of the fairy tale of the elves and the shoemaker. Using the Internet to run and manage its operations, the project aims to change the urban environment and, through doing so, improve people's well-being. Volunteers are brought together via the Guerrilla Gardening website and meet in the middle of the night to quietly clean up an urban area and plant flowers, bushes, and trees. When the local residents wake up, they find themselves in a beautifully transformed landscape. This project started in London, and its success has led to the formation of similar projects in many major cities around the world, including New York, Berlin, and Toronto. The recruitment of volunteers and operational logistics are carried out via the Internet, but the activity itself occurs entirely offline.

Another example is Illinois Legal Aid Online (ILAO), an organization that seeks to provide justice for people who cannot afford to pay legal fees. For those on low incomes, it provides legal information, and professional advice in any field and has provided legal aid for more than 3 million people. In contrast to Guerilla Gardening, its activities are carried out purely online.

Many websites allow potential volunteers to sign up for projects located all over the world. Geographical distance is irrelevant on the Internet.

WHAT SPECIAL ADVANTAGES DOES ONLINE VOLUNTEERING OFFER?

I (Amichai-Hamburger, 2008) analyzed online versus offline volunteering and suggested that online volunteering has some major advantages on the individual, interpersonal, group, and overall self-actualization levels.

Let's start with the advantages that exist on the individual level.

INDIVIDUAL LEVEL

People wonder whether they have anything to offer as a volunteer if they have only limited time available. They question how one person can make a significant difference in relation to the world's many problems, and indeed if online volunteering is even worthwhile. The best response to these musings is that the flexibility granted by the Internet allows everyone to volunteer for a project of their choice, in whatever capacity best suits them. *Individual flexibility* coupled with the advantages of the Internet means we can all take the opportunity to do good. People can also decide to start their own online projects. Volunteering online gives participants the opportunity to find the best fit between their own needs and abilities and those of a relevant project. Most of us have knowledge and skills that can be utilized. For example, imagine that you are studying organizational psychology at university. Around the world are many people who could benefit from your knowledge, such as those wanting to know how to improve the group dynamics of their grassroots political organization. It doesn't matter where your skills lie – whether you have knowledge of plumbing or organizing a household budget; are fluent in Spanish and Swahili; or can knit a cardigan – your knowledge is valuable to someone, somewhere in the world. Here are a few examples of ways in which you can help people online:

- *Develop an online learning environment* – Many people have the knowledge and skills needed to develop a teaching and learning website. Consider a website for helping people improve their spoken and written English. Many people around the world need to master the English language, as it is a key to acquiring valuable knowledge and getting a better job.
- *Legal aid* – Legal knowledge is always relevant. Say, for example, that you have a qualification in international business law. A small business in a poor country that is seeking to expand but needs help understanding the global environment would certainly benefit from your expertise.
- *Fundraising* – Lots of good causes need funding to get them off the ground. You may be able to help them apply for grants from established charitable foundations, or you may have a useful personal

contact, or you may be able to design a website that helps collect donations from the public.

* *Marketing* – PR and marketing experts can help an online organization identify, frame, and publicize its vision so that it targets the intended audience.

How prosocial we perceive ourselves to be is an important component of how we see ourselves as people, our *individual self-definition*. We ask ourselves at different stages of life whether we are sufficiently altruistic. Many people will answer negatively based on the fact that they have simply not found the time in their busy lives to volunteer and do some good. Some people are concerned about the time commitment involved in a voluntary project, and will therefore avoid it altogether. Online volunteering may make them feel less pressured. They can try out the experience before making a decision to commit. This knowledge makes people braver and more willing to chance getting involved. On the Internet, people know they can leave, which, paradoxically, makes them more inclined to enjoy the experience of belonging to a particular online project and eventually to commit themselves to it.

One great example of how online volunteering can change people's individual self-definition is seen in the participation of those with special needs. For many, the experience of volunteering online is transformative – turning them from people who are dependent on others to people who give to others. This is an amazing psychological change. The person with special needs may well not self-identify as someone with a disability, and an online project may represent a unique opportunity to be judged solely on the worth of their contribution, with no other mitigating factors involved. This may encourage such individuals to further change their own self-definition to something more empowering and positive.

This very important dynamic was recognized by Ad de Raad, former United Nations Volunteers Executive Coordinator, when he stated: "We believe that volunteerism and volunteers represent the first and the last mile of connectivity. In particular, online volunteerism creates new opportunities for people who have too often been excluded from participation – such as older volunteers, people with disabilities, individuals living in remote areas, and those with pressing domestic responsibilities or very limited means."

The next section focuses on volunteers themselves, using direct quotations from inspiring people all over the world regarding what online volunteering means to them. As you read, note how the act of online volunteering impacted on the way that the volunteers saw themselves. For those interested in learning more and perhaps getting involved, the web addresses of various online organizations are provided in the Notes at the end of this chapter.

Emmanuel Owobu, a member of an online team, who among many amazing things drafted an eye-care plan that serves several villages in rural Nigeria, says, "Volunteering for Delta Women has really given me much more than I anticipated. I always felt I could do more to help both people within my immediate surroundings and others not within my reach."[1]

Online volunteer Leonardo Parrado Varón is a member of the Asociación Aprendo Contigo ("I Learn with You"), a Peruvian non-profit organization that delivers educational services to children and young people undergoing medical treatment. For him, "An illness should not be grounds for solitude and neglect, and even less when it comes to children. I am still young but have never had the strength to give anything more than good intentions. I hope that amongst the children I helped, someday one will achieve something great, perhaps the cure for cancer or a solution to hunger. This could be the result of 'education and opportunities' – at least I hope so."[2]

Another volunteer, Slawosz Fliegner, a German Business Administration graduate, says: "Online volunteering gives me the ability to contribute, as opposed to simply donate. Contribution is a team effort and a form of dialogue, which allows you to help in solving a problem. By volunteering online I can go beyond the notion of charity and work on a project to the best of my abilities to create a social impact."[3]

INTERPERSONAL LEVEL

Online volunteering is a great place to meet similar others – people who care about society and have chosen a similar means of doing good. Therefore, it should be no surprise that online projects have been shown to be great springboards for the development of significant *friendships*. As Stanley Tuvako, an online volunteer for Kenya AIDS Intervention and Prevention Project (KAIPPG), explained, "I have learned to be a friend and have felt like those I have worked with have appreciated my friendship. I have made friends with the world, while the world has made friends with me. I have learned to give and be pleased about it" (quoted in Amichai-Hamburger, 2008).

Kirthi Jayakumar, a young lawyer from India and member of an online group carrying out research on the entrepreneurial environment in African countries, says, "I built a personal relationship with most of the volunteers who I coordinated, and today I can safely say I have become richer by many friends."[4]

Moreover, online volunteering can very easily lead to the formation of romantic relationships. Working with someone who shares your ideals and values can result in finding a soulmate.

When the interaction, at least at the beginning, lacks exposure to physical appearance, it enables interpersonal relationships to flow, free from the constraints of stereotypical thinking. Working on a prosocial project with people who share your values changes the salience and relevance of background differences and *counters reliance on stereotypes*. In online projects, the contribution of each member is judged on the basis of objective criteria regarding how much it helped group goals, rather than on a subjective stereotypical basis.

As described earlier in the book, people who are socially inhibited are likely to seek *social compensation* online (Amichai-Hamburger & Hayat, 2013). In the protected online environment, they are more likely to adopt a different persona and to act in an extrovert manner. Online volunteering projects, in which they work with similar others who share similar ideals, may be the ideal place for introverts to recreate themselves and express themselves more freely.

GROUP IDENTITY

Being with others who think like you, for example on environmental issues, can have a positive effect on how you feel about yourself as a person. Becoming part of an offline group is often a long process, but online you can feel a sense of acceptance quite quickly. Group membership may make you feel powerful and confident. Again, these ideas are best expressed by volunteers themselves.

Sandrine Cortet is an online volunteer for a website producing French courses for people who cannot afford formal secondary education. She now manages a team of fifty volunteers, and says: "Online volunteering gives the opportunity to be involved in completely different universes and to meet amazingly talented and dedicated people from all over the world working on the same project while everyone is distant. Life is short and it is not enough time to build a perfect world, but at least we can try to make it better" (Amichai-Hamburger, 2008).

What we are seeing here is synergy – a whole that is more than the sum of its parts. In those groups where members are deeply committed to group goals, people tend to give their best. This can produce outstanding results that not only benefit the beneficiaries of such prosocial groups, but also the group as a whole and its members as individuals. Members frequently feel lucky and blessed to belong to such groups.

A group dedicated to helping others is likely to adhere to positive and kind norms. Group members are likely to receive positive reinforcement for their efforts. When this kind of positive group is available 24 hours a day, each group member's identity as an online volunteer is likely to become an increasingly significant part of their identity, and so have a positive impact on their well-being.

SOLVING THE CONFLICT BETWEEN THE DESIRE FOR AUTONOMY AND THE NEED TO BELONG

The simultaneous need for autonomy and group membership (Fromm, 1941) is a central existential conflict in human experience. Earlier, we suggested that the Internet, with its endless groups and the feeling of protection and empowerment it engenders, creates an environment in which this conflict can easily be resolved (Amichai-Hamburger, 2008). I would like to suggest that online volunteering groups represent the peak of this resolution. Volunteers can develop their own individuality while also being part of a significant group of like-minded, possibly high achieving, others. This is expressed succinctly by Will Wallace, a US online volunteer, who offers IT support for RESPECT (Refugee Education Sponsorship Program: Enhancing Communities Together): "As an online volunteer, you get to work with some of the best people you will never meet. Together you will make a difference in the world. And your skills, no matter what they are, are just the ones someone has been looking for" (Amichai-Hamburger, 2008).

Or consider the work of online volunteer Elisabeth Fernandez-Begault, who wrote a series of standard contracts to be used with various counterparts, thereby strengthening the administrative and legal framework of Benin-based NGO, Fondation Joseph the Worker, which works to protect people from torture. An attorney specializing in public law and a university lecturer, Elisabeth says, "Collaborating with the organization was excellent, with very productive and responsive online exchanges. Volunteering has inspired my professional life. Being an online volunteer is a source of pride."[5]

SELF-ACTUALIZATION

Here, we will discuss the self-actualization that results from making this type of contribution. Although this section does indeed overlap with the individual level discussed above, it also represents something so much greater and more profound that we have decided to devote a section to it.

The well-known psychologist Abraham Maslow (1908–1970) believed that when human beings have achieved their basic survival needs of food, shelter, and so on, they will then strive for self-actualization. We believe that the Internet allows more people than ever before to achieve their self-actualization. Moreover, it appears that there are important similarities among individuals who reach a high degree of self-actualization, as defined by Maslow, and those who get involved in online projects promoting social change. Maslow suggests that people who are problem-centered – meaning that they treat life's difficulties as problems demanding solutions, not as personal troubles to be remonstrated with or surrendered to – are those who are most likely to reach self-actualization. He believed that such people have a sense of humility and respect for others (what he defined as human kinship or social interest), compassion, humanity, and democratic values (meaning they are open to individual differences and actually value them); they are people who treasure their autonomy and feel a relative independence from physical and social needs. Maslow believed that these qualities are accompanied by a strong ethical belief system that may well be spiritual, but is seldom conventionally religious in nature. He believed that such people enjoy more peak experiences than the average person. A peak experience is one in which you are totally involved, making you feel that you are a part of the infinite and possibly eternal – at one with life, nature, or God. People who have experienced such a thing feel that they have been changed for the better, and many people actively seek out peak experiences.

Interestingly, many online volunteers themselves refer to their voluntary contribution as an expression of their self-actualization.

The Ann Foundation is an active group of online volunteers from all over the globe, which has been developing and teaching daily online classes in various languages to children with visual or hearing disabilities across eight cities in India. The work of the Ann Foundation has empowered over 2,000 children.

Cheryl Stafford, a US teacher and disability services professional, works as a volunteer for the Ann Foundation. She discovered online volunteering in 2011, while recovering from medical treatment herself: "I met many people, from an impoverished student with disabilities striving for independence, to statesmen, business executives, and famous celebrities. So from my lifetime home in a quiet rural corner, my world has grown to include the experiences of volunteers around the globe, the hopes and dreams of countless children and youth in other countries."[6]

Mohammad Ashaq Malik from India has completed approximately twenty voluntary assignments, writing and carrying out research. He echoes the notion that volunteering can lead to self-actualization, saying, "There are people in this world who want to do something good in life…. The Online Volunteering service is a great platform to serve humankind and get experience, inner satisfaction and enjoyment as well" (Amichai-Hamburger, 2008).

Overall, we can see how those who use the Internet to volunteer for worthwhile projects are able to make a difference in countless lives, including their own.

HOW CAN THE INTERNET REDUCE AGGRESSION BETWEEN COUNTRIES AND COMMUNITIES?

We will now consider how the Internet is relevant to one of the most painful realities of the world we live in: war and aggression between groups, communities, and states. Psychologists use the term intergroup (as opposed to individual) conflict to refer to this state of affairs, and this section does so too. Below, we will discuss the leading process advocated for resolving intergroup conflict and suggest that the Internet has an important role to play.

INTERGROUP CONFLICT: BRINGING RIVAL GROUPS TOGETHER

Intergroup conflict is taking place all over the world, causing huge amounts of pain and destruction and incurring high economic costs. In 1954, Gordon Allport, a social psychologist, suggested that if representatives of the rival parties met under certain stipulated circumstances, the chances of reaching a rapprochement would considerably increase. Allport called his idea the Contact Hypothesis, and it has become very well known; in fact, it has been described as one of the most successful ideas in the history of social psychology (Brown, 2000). Allport's ideas were based on his understanding that true acquaintance lessens prejudice. Think about it: intellectual understanding alone will not cause people to abandon their prejudices and review the stereotypes they attribute to others because, in all likelihood, they will only accept those pieces of information that fit into their fixed world view. Countering prejudice and stereotyping can only be achieved by getting to know "others" as individuals.

Allport defined four key conditions for a meeting ("contact," in his terminology) between two sides in a conflict: (1) the representatives of each side should have equal group status; (2) they should agree on common goals; (3) they should build intergroup cooperation to achieve those superordinate goals; and (4) they should receive institutional support for their group. Several other conditions were later added, the most important of these being voluntary participation and intimate contact (Amir, 1969, 1976). There is strong empirical support demonstrating that, when effectively implemented, the conditions described above do indeed lead to a positive attitude change that is target-specific (e.g., Brown & Wade, 1987). The evidence, however, is less clear regarding global attitude changes.

Pettigrew and Tropp (2000) examined the results of contact studies carried out on the basis of the Contact Hypothesis. They reported that bias may be reduced, even in cases when not all of Allport's stipulations have been met. In fact, the mere contact between individuals from both sides can be a sufficient condition for the long-term reduction of prejudice. Not only are the individuals who took part in the contact affected, but the effect also generalizes to their larger group. However, each of Allport's conditions does play an important role in helping to reduce prejudice and stereotypical thinking – the greater the number of conditions that are present, the more likely it is that contact will achieve a successful and lasting outcome.

MINI-BIOGRAPHY: GORDON ALLPORT

Gordon Allport (1897–1967) was a humanistic psychologist whose career was spent mainly in the psychology department at Harvard University. His father was a village doctor and Allport's childhood home was characterized by giving and helping those in need. Allport's childhood was not easy – he was a shy child, born with only four toes, and teased by other children.

His career path was formed in a surprising way, following a meeting with Freud. At this meeting, Allport told Freud about a small incident involving a child that he had witnessed on his train journey to Vienna. Freud turned suddenly to Allport and asked him a question, which was actually a statement of fact: "This little child is you?" Allport was considerably shocked by what he perceived as the oversimplicity of Freud's explanation, and this encounter would become a seminal event for him, causing him to follow a distinctly different route to that of Freud. Allport was to state, later in his career, that Freudian theory sees the vile passions of the subconscious as the essence of each human being, while it largely ignores consciousness. Allport chose to focus his research on healthy people, concentrating on how the unique parts of an individual interact with the specific context that that individual operates within. He focused his personality theory on the systematic study of traits, whereas Freud focused on instincts. Allport's book, *Personality: A Psychological Interpretation* (1937), is considered a seminal work, which lead to the topic of personality officially becoming part of the study of psychology. His work has had considerable influence on the development of important and widely used personality questionnaires, such as those identifying the Big Five traits (extraversion, agreeableness, openness, conscientiousness, and neuroticism). Allport saw shortcomings in the prevailing schools of psychological thought of his day: psychoanalysis over-analyzed people, while behaviorism ignored the unique qualities of each individual. He felt that humanistic psychology represented a golden middle path between the two.

In 1954, Allport played a major role in assisting the US Supreme Court reach its verdict on race equality. He helped to design the new policy of integration in the US educational system. From this point onwards, he devoted his life to improving the relations between groups in strife. His formative book in this field, *The Nature of Prejudice* (1954), has been reprinted twenty-five times.

Although proven successful, for both logistical and economic reasons Allport's conditions are actually challenging to put in place. In fact, even arranging for a simple meeting may prove exceptionally difficult if the warring factions would lose face were they seen meeting together. Two major obstacles are faced by people wishing to hold contact meetings, according to the Contact Hypothesis. These are, first, the *practicality issue*. Contact between rival groups according to the conditions required by the Contact Hypothesis might be very complicated to arrange and expensive to run. This is particularly true when you consider that few disputes are solved in a single meeting, and factor in the logistics of individual timetables and the potentially prohibitive expense of flying both groups to a neutral location. The second obstacle is *anxiety*. Despite the fact that attendance at the contact meeting is voluntary, there is likely to be a high degree of anxiety among participants, as a result of being in close physical proximity to their enemy (or "outgroup members," in psychological terms). This anxiety leads people (often against their conscious will) to apply stereotypical and prejudiced thinking to the other side of the conflict. These factors, sadly, are likely to reduce the probability that the contact meeting will be a success (Amichai-Hamburger & McKenna, 2006).

HOW CAN THE INTERNET PLAY A PART IN INTERGROUP CONTACT?

In 2006, I wrote a paper with Katlyn McKenna (Amichai-Hamburger & McKenna, 2006) in which we put forward the idea that if inter-group contact was held online, it would be possible to uphold all of Allport's stipulations with none of the ensuing obstacles. For example, one of Allport's conditions is that the participants from the two sides are of equal status. This can be a real challenge because one of the main differences between many rival groups *is* their social status, and, in some cases, is the source of the conflict itself. When the contact is held offline, these differences in wealth and status are often salient. Holding the contact meeting offline is likely to emphasize differences in appearance, social status, and so on. Online, however, these details are much less significant. As we have empha-sized throughout this book, people feel a greater sense of equality online, as social status symbols are not part of the interaction. This is likely to create a more positive atmosphere in the contact meeting. Another difficulty that can be countered online is the complexity involved in staging a contact meeting in neutral territory acceptable to both parties. Holding a meeting in cyberspace resolves automati-cally both the logistic and economic issues. Moreover, because of the low costs involved, meetings may be held as many times and as often as necessary. In fact, because of the cost factor, many offline contact projects that were actually successful did not lead to predicted long-term changes because budgetary constraints prevented further meet-ings to reinforce those changes. As online intergroup contact is so much cheaper, rival groups can follow-up on their successes, and so enhance the likelihood that the project will have a long-term posi-tive impact. Those are just a few examples of how online contact can solve many of the offline contact logistical issues.

Furthermore, anxiety is likely to be reduced significantly as people feel much more protected if they take part in the contact from a known, secure environment. Offline, this is unlikely to happen, since a face-to-face meeting would most likely increase feelings of appre-hension among participants from both sides, particularly if both groups are involved in a deeply rooted and violent conflict. When offline, the anxiety felt by participants regarding the reaction of the other outgroup members makes it more likely that they will resort to old stereotypes, thus reducing the likelihood of the contact having a positive outcome. However online, anxiety is reduced, and people are likely to be more open regarding what happens in the contact meeting and so the likelihood of success is higher.

In 2009, I took this idea a stage further, and proposed the setting-up of an online intergroup contact platform. My idea was that, as part of online contact, participants from both sides should build a data bank containing details of their cultural norms and codes of behavior. This should be studied by the other group members before the contact meeting, and it could also be utilized in real time during the meeting to avoid cultural misunderstandings. For example, a group member from a more liberal culture would be able to avoid an inappropriate interaction with a female member from the outgroup who may come from a more religious, traditional society. Importantly, my platform included a moderator, who had to be a social psychologist specifically trained in this field. This moderator would make sure that online discussions were held in a respectful way, and would have the power to punish participants who violated the rules of conduct. These ideas have since influenced major projects in this field.

Below we focus on two important projects in the field of online intergroup contact.

ONLINE CONTACT BETWEEN CATHOLIC AND PROTESTANT CHILDREN IN IRELAND

Dissolving Boundaries, run from a university in Northern Ireland and a university in the Republic of Ireland, is one of the most extensively studied and well-documented online intergroup contact projects. Following decades of violent conflict between Catholics and Protestants, it aims to form a bridge between children from these communities. The program pairs schools – one Protestant and one Catholic – and arranges for small groups of pupils to link up. While remaining in their own environments, children from both schools participate in collaborative online activities. These have been shown to facilitate cross-community links and to have a positive overall impact. Teachers report that those children who participate showed an increased respect and tolerance for opposing views and a greater understanding of the other side. The perception of ingroup/out-group similarity is also enhanced, particularly in the case of primary school pupils. Younger pupils also report that the programme helps them to develop cross-group friendships, more so than is the case for older pupils. This indicates that these types of contact are most effective with young people probably because they are more open to the process.

Both the schools as institutions and the teachers as authorities must support the program, because such support has been identified as a crucial factor in its success. Roger Austin, who coordinates the program on the Northern Ireland side of the divide, stressed that teachers' enthusiasm is critical for the success of an online intergroup encounter, but is insufficient if the aspirations of the program are not supported by the participating schools. He also recommends avoiding sensitive topics – at least in the initial phase (Austin, 2006).

ONLINE CONTACT BETWEEN ISRAELI JEWISH AND MUSLIM STUDENT TEACHERS

This project was set up by the Centre for Multiculturalism and Technology for religious and secular Jewish and Arab teacher training colleges in Israel. It is an online, educational project with the objective of teaching prospective educators to master educational technologies effectively, and to provide them with the opportunities to experience a whole variety of cultures and viewpoints in the hope that this perspective will influence their own careers as school teachers. The studies take place under the online supervision of trained instructors, as participants from the different communities work collaboratively online while remaining in their own physical settings.

This project is described in detail by Hoter et al. (2012). Their appraisal of the project revealed that the participants were highly appreciative of the whole program, particularly the multicultural learning experience, and they had formed strong connections with the other members of their group. In addition, students reported that they had learned that their own group actually had far more in common with the other group than they previously realized and that they could identify with the outgroup members as a result of this learning experience. After carefully assessing their findings on the project, Hoter et al. concluded that structured online intergroup contact interventions "can reduce bias, stigmas, and ethnic prejudice among prospective teachers" (ibid., 10).

When we examine the major components of the project, we can further understand its success. First, the project focused on long-term collaboration; second, the organizers ensured that the meetings started as text-based contacts only, thus reducing many of the social stereotypes and prejudices we spoke of earlier. Gradually, as trust and confidence grew, meetings progressed from text messages to audio/video channels, and finally to face-to-face meetings. Third, it concentrated on general rather than controversial topics. (This, by the way, is a major accomplishment in such a charged region.) Fourth, organizers employed course instructors from different cultural groups.

The tactic of progressing from less-revealing media (e.g., texting) to final face-to-face meetings has been shown to be an effective way to reduce anxiety in the initial phases of the contact. In this case, the organizers were particularly aware of the sensitivities of the Arab students who were at a disadvantage since communication took place in Hebrew, which is not their first language; a policy was thus instituted whereby all spelling errors were to be ignored.

WHAT HAPPENS WHEN ONLINE INTERGROUP CONTACT IS ALLOWED TO RUN FREE?

An almost infinite number of intergroup contacts are taking place via the Internet at any given time, in the form of forums, social networking sites, and so on. What these groups have in common is that they are not operating under the auspices of formal institutions nor are they guided by facilitators. In fact, Ruesch (2011) analyzed 770 Facebook groups based around the Israel–Palestine conflict, and then pointed out that most of them were extremely radical in tone and under 15 percent defined themselves as peace-seeking groups dedicated to intergroup dialogue and peace initiatives. Members of these extremist groups tended to express hateful, antagonistic opinions, almost completely devoid of interest in or empathy for any of the positions held by their opponents. This supports the finding of Amichai-Hamburger and McKenna (2006), that successful contact needs to be structured and supervised, because an unstructured environment is likely to invite conflict and heighten tensions.

Another exciting, if perhaps unexpected, avenue for improving intergroup relations is online games, as described in the next section.

CAN ONLINE GAMES PROMOTE BETTER INTERGROUP RELATIONS?

Many people spend time playing games on the Internet. So it's worth considering how they might be harnessed as a means of improving intergroup relationships. One way is through realistic encounter games, where participants find themselves taking part in a conflict scenario representing one party. This direct approach enables people who are involved in a conflict to gain a greater understanding of the issues that divide them and find innovative ways to reach a solution. Since the game allows participants to see their conflict from many different perspectives, they may well become more objective; therefore, these online games serve as a formidable learning tool. The games can also serve as a platform for people not involved directly in a specific conflict to understand it more deeply and develop conflict resolution skills. The second kind of game is based around individual skills. In this case, an environment is designed that includes situations either imaginary or unrelated to the participants. The aim of the game is to challenge the players' ways of thinking and help them develop skills that will eventually aid in solving the intergroup conflict. It is intended that the knowledge and insights acquired in the game will be transferred to real life.

A good example of a game designed to reduce intergroup conflict is *PeaceMaker*.[7] It can teach us a lot about the challenges involved in creating such games, and the components necessary for them to have a positive impact. The game focuses on the Israeli–Palestinian conflict, and enables a single player to assume the roles of the Israeli prime minister or the Palestinian president and to bring about a resolution of the crisis by using political, economic, and security measures. Kampf (2014) assessed what happened when the game was played solo or in pairs (dyads) comprising Jewish and Arab students. The dyads were required to reach agreement on every action. Perhaps surprisingly, Kampf found that dyads resolved more conflicts than did single players. Through his own observations and interviews conducted with players, Kampf demonstrated that, as a result of playing *PeaceMaker* and partaking in interaction around it, both Arab and Jewish players felt that they had gained new information about the conflict. However, Kampf's conclusions also specified that the dialogues conducted between the players showed that considerations such as the desire to win the game or the need to arrive at an agreed-upon decision regarding every action had directed the cooperation. This indicates that people may differentiate between their real opinions and those they express in the game. I believe that the main impact of these games stems from a combination of fun and learning. It is therefore important to stress that, although it is a significant game, *PeaceMaker* was released in 2007, which in gaming years makes it ancient – in order for the game to continue to have an impact, it needs a major upgrade. In other words, games that are more dynamic and attractive have a greater chance of managing to bring about a change in the nature of the intergroup conflict.

The Internet thus appears to have a great deal to offer to people who wish to improve intergroup relations. Unfortunately, this huge potential remains largely untapped.

WHAT ADDITIONAL ONLINE TOOLS CAN WE USE TO REDUCE STEREOTYPICAL THINKING AND IMPROVE INTERGROUP RELATIONSHIPS?

The answer to this question will focus on three innovative and futuristic ideas: identity enrichment; online intergroup role-playing; and training online change agents.

IDENTITY ENRICHMENT

Although it sounds complex, the idea of the identity enrichment (IE) online platform is quite simple. Its basic premise is that, if we can broaden the way people see themselves (that is, their identity), then they will be able to find things in common with a greater number of people and, equally important, acquire self-esteem from a variety of sources, some of which they probably would not have considered before. Simply put, IE is a web platform that enables people to specify their interests and hobbies and then directs them to online groups to interact with others like them. The idea is that interacting in online groups helps individuals to broaden their identities, and exposes them to people outside their own ethnic group, with the expectation that such encounters might help them to relate well to outgroup members face to face.

This platform is an educational online tool for children, based on the premise that they will transfer their broadened, more complex identity into their adult lives. IE is particularly interesting in that it makes no specific reference to the outgroup, and concentrates only on enriching the self-definition of its users. By doing so, the platform seeks to improve relations with the outgroup indirectly, eventually equipping its users with many possibilities to create common ground with outgroup members in the future.

To understand how an IE platform aids intergroup relations, it's important to say a few words about self-esteem. Identity is strongly connected to self-esteem and, according to social identity theory (SIT; Tajfel & Turner, 1986), we are motivated to increase it. One way to achieve this, of course, is through our own achievements, but another is by being part of a group. Group membership, however, can result in making "social comparisons"; that is, we compare our group (the "ingroup") to a relevant outgroup, and find the ingroup superior. Social comparisons are an important element of our self-esteem. When seeking to improve intergroup relations, one pivotal challenge is to identify how people can reduce the need to enhance their self-esteem through ingroup favoritism (social comparisons) and, instead, acquire it from a variety of other sources. As an online process, this involves gaining confidence in their own worth and abilities by belonging to groups of similar-minded people who share their interests and hobbies, rather than seeking approval from members of their core group (family, coworkers, and so on) in their daily lives. Although aimed at children, this game, or similar, may serve an important role in the lives of adolescents.

As previously mentioned, Erikson (1968) believed that the major challenge during the adolescent stage of development is finding the answer to the all-pervasive question, "Who am I?" A game may serve as a means for a young person to work through the process of answering this question. And, in a larger sense, the ability to experience different parts of one's identity through the Internet may also help them reach a satisfactory answer. The main benefit the IE process offers would thus seem to be that it enables individuals to enrich their identities. Today, through the Internet, we can find similar others all over the world; we are no longer limited to our core group. Interestingly, there is evidence, much of it anecdotal, of widespread connections between members of opposing groups through the Internet. As one Israeli man recently related at a dinner-party, "I am in close touch with people in Gaza and Saudi Arabia; we use Google translate and write to each other in English. We often longingly wish that we could visit one another in our homes…. When people ask me about making these connections, I always tell them, start with non-controversial things, things you have in common. I usually start with siblings, but you can certainly talk about sport, like English football. It is fascinating to note that, with no formal training, this man has recognized an important element of making successful contact, namely, starting with noncontroversial topics.

As their broader identity forms, people can use the IE platform to discover appropriate online groups that will help them to develop and reinforce much richer identities. Their interaction with other group members may also counter their stereotypical thinking because the connections formed online are based exclusively on a mutual interest, with no relevance to other issues such as the ethnic or religious group to which they belong. In this way, members can interact, exchange information, play, and form close connections, while suspending factors such as physical appearance, religion, and ethnic origin. These online groups, which are accessible everywhere, round the clock, are likely to become an important component in the self-esteem of their members.

ONLINE INTERGROUP ROLE-PLAYING

Role-playing games – games that allow users to engage in life-like scenarios online – can be very beneficial for improving intergroup relations. They enable us to learn how the other side perceives the world (Lamm, Batson & Decety, 2007), and they can also help us to develop skills that are relevant to our attitudes toward outgroup members, especially if one group is discriminated against by a higher status group. Online, through fantasy games, users are able to create a very realistic experience. *SecondLife*[8] is one such fantasy game. Here, players act through an avatar – a cartoon representation that they choose and control. Players can choose an avatar who looks like them or someone quite different, even an animal. As soon as a player has created an avatar, they are free to participate in individual and group activities. Researchers in the field of intergroup conflict found that, when Caucasian men and women interacted with one another in *SecondLife* while using African American avatars, they not only identified with their avatars, but also felt less negative attitudes toward the African-American community, and displayed more empathy, as compared with participants who played as Caucasian avatars.

This study demonstrates that being in the "body" of your rival, your enemy, or simply someone different to you in an online fantasy environment can influence your attitude toward others in the offline world. This finding is in line with results of studies carried out offline, which showed that taking someone else's perspective may help you to understand their point of view (Davis et al., 1996) and reduce stereotypical thinking about the group to which they belong (Galinsky & Moskowitz, 2000). Nick Yee and Jeremy Bailenson (2006) carried out a study in which people spent time as elderly people, that is, they became elderly people in *collaborative virtual environments* (CVEs). They found that, following this experience, participants expressed more positive feelings towards the elderly than they had done previously.

The virtual reality experience can clearly be very significant. In fact, in no other situation can an individual "get inside the skin" of another and closely experience how it is to interact as them. As Bailenson and Yee demonstrated, such an experience can influence later, offline, behavior. Virtual reality technology is making such games ever more real; soon web surfers will be able to smell, touch, and feel what they encounter online. Experiencing others in situations that are even closer to reality will greatly increase empathy and understanding on both sides. Using games to effect reconciliation between opposing parties may thus also result in greater success.

Another important development is the *virtual intergroup role-playing game*, the aim of which is to build a platform akin to that of the fantasy environment in *SecondLife*, but instead players have the opportunity to "step into the body" of an outgroup member. I hope to design a more controlled environment than that of *SecondLife*. My platform would allow people to encounter different situations – such as being discriminated against or being the victim of negative stereotyping – while "in the body" of an outgroup member. I believe that this experience will influence players' attitudes toward outgroups offline. This environment would be devised so as to create a whole range of experiences – such as direct and indirect discrimination – designed to teach skills relevant to conflict resolution.

TRAINING ONLINE CHANGE AGENTS

People's need to conform with those around them, and their vulnerability to peer pressure, may make them act in racist and discriminatory ways. (Although, I must note here that conformity can also have the opposite effect and actually be the cause of a decline in racist and stereotypical thinking.) Paluck (2011) examined the effect of training student leaders in methods for handling expressions of prejudice and harassment, based on the type of training provided by the Anti-Defamation League (ADL), an international Jewish NGO. The project has proven successful in positively affecting social networking norms. Setting up an online anti-prejudice leadership training program based on that of the ADL is one of the best ways in which to influence group attitudes. Such a program would supply participants with the knowledge and skills necessary to empathize with others. Opinion leaders from a variety of websites could complete an online course similar to that of the ADL, but adapted to the Internet situation. They could then be asked to make practical use of their leadership position and skills to actively counter stereotyping, prejudice, and discrimination in the virtual world. Placing influential people in the center of the program, we believe, would create a snowball effect, leading to an increasingly positive impact throughout cyberspace.

A FINAL WORD

In this chapter, we have looked at many different ways in which the Internet allows us to have a positive impact on the world, and, in the process, on ourselves. Endless opportunities and options exist out there in cyberspace, and if none of them are the perfect fit, there is always the possibility of starting your own prosocial project. The endless variety of online activities – from volunteering websites to games that foster connection between hostile groups – means that everyone can find something that fits their personality and abilities. Despite the challenges and hazards the Internet presents, it's worth remembering that it can so often be an avenue for good, providing powerful approaches for changing the world, one click at a time.

NOTES

1 www.onlinevolunteering.org/en/blog/delta-women-team
2 www.onlinevolunteering.org/en/blog/asociación-aprendo-contigo-team
3 www.onlinevolunteering.org/en/blog/association-african-entrepreneurs-team
4 www.onlinevolunteering.org/en/blog/association-african-entrepreneurs-team
5 www.onlinevolunteering.org/en/blog/fondation-joseph-worker-team
6 www.onlinevolunteering.org/en/blog/ann-foundation-team
7 www.peacemakergame.com
8 www.secondlife.com

REFERENCES

Allport, G. W. (1937). *Personality: A Psychological Interpretation*. New York: Holt, Rinehart, & Winston.

Allport, G. W. (1954). *The Nature of Prejudice*. Cambridge, MA: Addison-Wesley.

Amichai-Hamburger, Y. (2008). Potential and promise of online volunteering. *Computers in Human Behavior*, 24, 544–562.

Amichai-Hamburger, Y. (2013). Reducing intergroup conflict and promoting intergroup harmony in the digital age. In H. Giles (Ed.), *The Handbook of Intergroup Communication* (pp. 181–193). New York: Routledge.

Amichai-Hamburger, Y., & Hayat, Z. (2013). Personality and the Internet. In Y. Amichai-Hamburger (Ed.), *The Social Net: Understanding Our Online Behavior* (pp. 1–20). New York: Oxford University Press.

Amichai-Hamburger, Y., & McKenna, K. Y. A. (2006). The contact hypothesis reconsidered: Interacting via the Internet. *Journal of Computer-Mediated Communication*, 11(3). http://jcmc.indiana.edu/vol11/issue3/amichai- hamburger.html.

Amir, Y. (1969). Contact hypothesis in ethnic relations. *Psychological Bulletin*, 71, 319–342.

Amir, Y. (1976). The role of intergroup contact in change of prejudice and ethnic relations. In P. A. Katz (Ed.), *Towards the Elimination of Racism* (pp. 73–123). New York: Plenum Press.

Austin, R. (2006). The role of ICT in bridge-building and social inclusion: Theory, policy and practice issues. *European Journal of Teacher Education*, 29, 145–161.

Brown, R. J. (2000). *Group Processes: Dynamics within and between Groups*, 2nd edition. Oxford: Blackwell.

Brown, R. J., & Wade, G. S. (1987). Superordinate goals and intergroup behaviour: The effects of role ambiguity and status on intergroup attitudes and task performance. *European Journal of Social Psychology*, 17, 131–142.

Davis, M. H., Conklin, L., Smith, A., & Luce, C. (1996). Effect of perspective taking on the cognitive representation of persons: A merging of self and other. *Journal of Personality and Social Psychology*, 70, 713–726.

Erikson, E. H. (1968). *Identity: Youth and Crisis*. New York: Norton.

Fromm, E. (1941). *Escape from Freedom*. New York: Rinehart.

Galinsky, A. D., & Moskowitz, G. B. (2000). Perspective-taking: Decreasing stereotype expression, stereotype accessibility and in-group favoritism. *Journal of Personality and Social Psychology*, 78, 708–724.

Gonzales, A. L., Falisi, A., & Hancock, J. T. (2010). Decreasing racist attitudes through virtual play: Evidence of verbal perspective taking by white students when playing black avatars in second life chat. Paper presented at the *Annual Convention of the National Communication Association*. San Francisco, CA.

Hoter, E., Shonfeld, M., & Ganayem, A. N. (2012). TEC Center: Linking technology, education and cultural diversity. *I-manager's Journal of Educational Technology*, 9, 15–22.

Kampf, R. (2014). Are two better than one? Playing singly, playing in dyads in a computerized simulation of the Israeli–Palestinian conflict. *Computers in Human Behavior*, 32, 9–14.

Lamm, C., Batson, C. D., & Decety, J. (2007). The neural basis of human empathy: Effects of perspective-taking and cognitive appraisal. *Journal of Cognitive Neuroscience*, 19, 42–58.

Ruesch, M. (2011) A peaceful net? Intergroup contact and communicative conflict resolution of the Israel–Palestine conflict on Facebook. Paper presented at the First Global Conference on Communication and Conflict, Prague.

Paluck, E. L. (2011). Peer pressure against prejudice: A high school field experiment examining social network change. *Journal of Experimental Social Psychology*, 47, 350–358.

Pettigrew, T. F., & Tropp, L. R. (2000). Does intergroup contact reduce prejudice? Recent meta-analytic findings. In S. Oskamp (Ed.), *Reducing Prejudice and Discrimination: Social Psychological Perspectives* (pp. 93–114). Mahwah, NJ: Erlbaum.

Spacapan, S., & Oskamp, S. (1992) *Helping and Being Helped*. Newbury Park, CA: Sage.

Stephan, W. G., & Stephan, C. W. (1985). Intergroup anxiety. *Journal of Social Issues*, 41, 157–175.

Tajfel, H., & Turner, J. C. (1986). The social identity theory of intergroup behavior. In S. Worchel & W. G. Austin (Eds.), *Psychology of intergroup relations* (pp. 7–24). Chicago, IL: Nelson-Hall.

Yee, N., & Bailenson, J. (2006). Walk a mile: The impact of direct perspective-taking on the reduction of negative stereotyping in immersive virtual environments. Presentation at the 9th Annual International Workshop on Presence, Cleveland, OH.

8

HOW DO WE SUCCESSFULLY NAVIGATE OUR WAY THROUGH THE DIGITAL JUNGLE?

Let's start with a story made famous by the seminal self-help book, *Seven Habits of Highly Effective People* by Stephen Covey (1989). On a foggy night two ships appear to be on a collision course and a dialogue ensues regarding which one should change direction to avert disaster. The captain of one repeatedly orders the crew of the other to move and becomes increasingly irate when they refuse. Ultimately it is revealed that the other 'vessel' is, in fact, a lighthouse. The captain duly changes direction.

Covey's insightful message is revealed if we consider the different components of the story as metaphors. I suggest that the ship represents us, regular people trying to live our lives in an unclear and sometimes tempestuous digital world in which we sometimes feel powerless. The storm and fog represent the idea that the only "stable" element in our lives is constant change and associated uncertainty and confusion. To be able to live a life of real meaning, we need to define our lighthouse of values and behave according to it.

In this chapter we will be asking some pertinent questions related to our values and sense of well-being.

WHAT ARE OUR PRIMARY CULTURAL VALUES AND HOW DO THEY AFFECT US?

The advancement of technology and its utilization is strongly influenced by the dominant culture in which it is being developed. This is actually a two-way street, as technology both influences culture and is influenced by it. Western culture has many values, among which three are particularly dominant: individuality; efficiency – time equals money; and materialism – I am what I can buy.

INDIVIDUALITY

Individuality is the ability to have a character that is unique and distinguished from others. Humanistic psychology advocates that each person is born with a unique potential. We have to strive to fulfill our special potential. To do so, we have to go through a long, challenging, and continual process of growth. Humanistic psychology advocates the importance of offering individuals a great deal of freedom to express themselves and develop in their own unique ways. Certainly, we tell ourselves that individuality is a central value of our society; however, some might say that our emphasis on individuality is all talk, and that in fact western society is much more conformist than it would have us believe.

A short scene in the 1979 film, *Life of Brian*, may provide illumination on this topic. The title character has inadvertently accumulated a large crowd of followers who believe him to be the messiah. Brian tries to rid them of their misconception and begs them to leave him alone. He attempts to convince them that they are all individuals and don't have to follow anyone. However his words have a reverse impact, as the whole crowd begins shouting in unison, mechanically repeating his own words back to him. This scene delivers the clear message that individuality can very easily become conformity – the complete opposite of individuality.

As stated earlier, humanistic psychology advocates self-actualization while acknowledging that it is a long process. However, contemporary western thought suggests that people can achieve individuality without hard work and effort. Rather, you can buy individuality in the form of a gadget, car, book, or pill. For example, just step into your local bookshop and no doubt you'll find a title along the lines of, "Ten steps to becoming a better…" No need to work hard any more. In fact, commercial companies have become experts at selling us individuality. "Buy this product and you will become a significant individual," declare their advertisements.

Individuality demands process. However, in the era of the Internet people seem to increasingly believe that process is no longer relevant in their lives. In fact, why would it have a place when in the space of five minutes spent on the net you can become an expert in almost any field imaginable. You can make multiple friends on Facebook with no effort at all. A romantic relationship can also be achieved almost instantaneously. This seemingly successful, instant way of thinking actually contradicts the concept of individuality.

CHATROOM: INDIVIDUALITY IN A BOTTLE

In 2014, Coca-Cola came up with a great campaign, "Share a Coke." They produced cans and bottles "personalized" with different first names such as Mary or Fred, in different languages across the world. As a result, people could buy a soft drink with their own name on it. Accordingly, people went to incredible lengths to source personalized cans for themselves, their children, their grandchildren, and so on. Later, the campaign moved to the Internet and people could purchase their "individual" can online. It gave buyers the feeling that the president of Coca-Cola, sitting in his office in Atlanta, had ordered his company to specially produce a unique Coca-Cola drink with their name on it. Had people stopped to think (something the company certainly didn't want to encourage), people would have realized that the campaign was ridiculous. Giving a mass-produced product a tiny personalized make-over was enough to make people believe that buying it enhanced their sense of individuality. This story teaches us two important things: first, how needy we are for individualism and, second, how easy it is to fool us.

EFFICIENCY – TIME IS MONEY

We live in an industrialized world which demands that individuals and organizations continuously become more efficient with their time. We are under constant pressure to do more and produce more. In organizations, workers have to demonstrate that they can produce more, of higher quality, in less time. For many of us, the separation between home and work no longer exists. We have forgotten that there was once a time when we left our place of work at 5 pm and didn't think about it until the next day. Most of us have portable computers and smartphones, which, when you think about it, are actually a form of handcuffs, ensuring that we don't escape from our "availability mode," that we are accessible "any time, any place, anywhere." Being practically at work all the time harms both our well-being and our relationships.

ENJOYING NATURE

A few years ago I visited a friend and colleague. He took me to a beautiful nature reserve and the scenery was stunning. However, beautiful though it was, my friend barely looked up from his smartphone. While I was enjoying the view of the lake, he was answering emails and organizing his meetings for the coming week. Much as I tried, and I was the guest, his behavior was preventing me from getting into the flow, feeling part of the scenery and enjoying my visit with him. After a while, I could bear it no longer, and asked him if he could pause for a bit and spend some time with me. He apologized, but explained that doing so was impossible. "No one gives me time-out," he said.

That much-needed escape known as "vacation-land" – a place of relaxation and forgetting about work – no longer exists for most of us, as more and more people admit that they work on holiday. Not being able to take time out makes people very vulnerable to burnout (Kane, 2015).

Furthermore, it's worth asking whether this pursuit of efficiency actually produces better work. The answer would appear to be, no, it does not. Amabile, Constance, and Kramer (2002) pointed out that creativity, an essential element of productivity, is stifled when subject to undue pressure. So really, what may seem like a good idea in the short term is actually having a detrimental effect on organizations in the long term.

MATERIALISM – I AM WHAT I CAN BUY

This is not a value that most people are aware of, and yet for many, it is the focus of their lives. Materialism refers to the need to accumulate material goods. Most people tend to measure their success using materialistic terms. I live in…, I own…, I bought…, and so on. What's more, the shopping mall seems to be a legitimate source of leisure activities.

Thus, we start defining ourselves based on what we own and what we can afford to buy. As this habit develops, our appetite for buying becomes insatiable, an existential hunger – we buy to prove that we exist.

At one time, advertisements were confined to specific, expected, spaces: on billboards or between programs on commercial television channels. Today, this is no longer the case; on the Internet we are inundated by ads. We are on the receiving end of an endless campaign, using both explicit and implicit ads, inviting us to buy and buy again. One typical online tactic is to create a sense of pressure in our buying. For example, many shopping websites stage a countdown or we find ourselves inadvertently competing with four other people who are interested in the same product. The message is clear: act now or miss out. In this case, individuality is translated into a promotion of goods, such as watches, cars, and gadgets. Again, the meaning is clear: purchase these products to become a sophisticated, distinct individual.

Another common Internet tactic encouraging us to buy without end is the use of offline and social network celebrities in in campaigns utilizing implicit persuasion on Instagram, Facebook, and Twitter. Generally, this means being exposed to ads without our being aware of it, and our ignorance of what we are really being exposed to makes it difficult to resist the message; we are caught with no psychological defenses. A viral campaign endorsed by big celebrities may well affect many of the people we interact with offline and online, thus making it even more unlikely that we will resist this underhanded approach.

Psychological research has shown that those who focus on materialistic achievements ("I simply have to own…") are less happy and content than unmaterialistic people (Kasser, 2002). Studies have shown that materialism is related to low levels of self-esteem, more conflict in our relationships, and a decline in sympathy (Kasser et al., 2004). In fact, studies have pointed out that the expression of sympathy for others is in decline in the western world (Twenge, 2013). It is also the case that, despite the standard of living having increased significantly in the western world – including our power to buy and our ability to secure a good education for our children – rates of depression are soaring. Seligmann (2002) suggested that all indices of anxiety and depression among young people are showing an increase as compared with previous generations.

We might ask ourselves: Is future technology going to lead us to a better place? One with less depression and loneliness? And a large dose of positive psychological well-being?

The materialistic society in which we live causes us to evaluate ourselves with shifting standards that always leave us feeling short changed. For example, we decide how well off we are based on the external criteria of comparisons with others. As a result, it is difficult to achieve happiness because we will always get used to a new luxury and, after a short time, treat it as a normative part of life. In addition, when we do well financially, we change our comparison group to one that is even wealthier, and are frustrated as a result.

Postman (1985) considered the form a future dictatorship might take. He pointed out that, while it was the book-burners who frightened George Orwell in his book *1984* (1949), in Aldous Huxley's *Brave New World* (1932), the real fear is felt the day after all the books have been confiscated – when people no longer wish to read at all. In Orwell's world, our freedom is taken by force; in Huxley's, it is removed without our even noticing. A clear example of the type of danger that Postman warned against may be seen in the sophistication of modern computer technology which has the capacity to learn the psychological profile of its users. This knowledge can help companies manipulate us with ever greater ease.

The companies that know most about us are probably Google and Facebook, and, as such, they have the greatest power to provide us (directly or indirectly) with "commercial individualism." They are the modern Big Brother, knowing almost all there is to know about us. Marissa Mayer, current president of Yahoo! and former executive at Google, many years ago claimed that Google knows more about individual web surfers than the individuals know about themselves.

Big Brother in the old world used power to gain control; in our modern world, we willingly give Big Brother the ability to control our lives.

Importantly, we can choose to take back control. We can do this by taking more control of our lives and enhancing our well-being. I believe that this can only begin to happen if we adopt a new set of values. This issue will be discussed in more detail towards the end of the chapter.

WHAT'S NEXT? THE CUTTING-EDGE TECHNOLOGICAL DEVELOPMENTS THAT WILL SOON CHANGE OUR LIVES FOREVER

There are many technological changes heading our way, which will alter the way we live, and they will be just as impactful as smartphones or Facebook – so get ready. Below we focus on four of them: robots, Internet of the five senses, inanimate objects online, and total documentation of action (i.e., what we do 24/7).

ROBOTS AND EMOTION

One of the most intriguing questions that has always surrounded the topic of robots is whether they will ever be on a par with human beings in terms of their intelligence, or if, perhaps, they might even surpass us. Today, the question has varied slightly, as scientists begin to examine robots and emotion. It is probably surprising for most people to learn that in the future we will have robots that can relate to people emotionally. They will be able to read emotions and express appropriate emotions in return. They will, for example, be able to understand that we are sad and in response will empathise.

INTERNET OF FIVE SENSES

The Internet is likely to continue to grow both in terms of the services it offers and the speed of delivery. Above all, the experience is likely to become more rewarding, and feel more real, as virtual reality technology continues to integrate with the Internet. So, how will it feel to surf the web in the future? Well, for starters, people will feel present in places they visit online, almost as if they are actually there. If you log into the Internet today and decide to pay a virtual visit to Niagara Falls, you will see the famous waterfall through several online cameras located at the site, and you may hear the sound of rushing water. In the future, a virtual visit to Niagara Falls will make you feel as though you are really there: feeling the weather conditions, smelling the air, experiencing the refreshing spray on your face. This will have great implications in the field of education, as pupils will be able to enjoy much more exciting and evocative learning experiences. Imagine, for example, being able to learn history from Ferdinand Magellan, the Portuguese explorer, as he describes the conditions of his sixteenth-century voyage, talking to him and being part of his adventures. The net experience will incorporate all five senses, including smell and touch.

INANIMATE OBJECTS ONLINE

In the future many of the objects and appliances that are part of our lives will be engaged in their own dialogues and group discussions, often without our intervention. From toasters to cars, the things we own will engage in an amazing network of objects – a system that will be able to help us run our lives efficiently, without our having to think too much about it. For example, such a system will make sure that we always have enough milk in the fridge; our car will route itself to the office automatically while we are on our smartphones preparing for the day's meetings.

TOTAL DOCUMENTATION OF ACTION

Already, we live lives that are intensely documented, in no small part due to social media. This trend will only increase, and soon it will be the case that almost everything will be documented, whether by computer, smartphone, or Internet cameras. We will be able to track our movements with the precision of moments.

So, do these developments make us better or worse off? This is a difficult question to answer. In relation to our psychological well-being, the impact will be multi-layered and complex. Like anything else, these changes are likely to bring with them both advantages and disadvantages. Take, for example, total documentation. Yes, significant benefits will accrue from this development, such as being able to integrate information from different sources. However, who will really be the great benefactor from such technologies? The answer is companies such as Google and Facebook. They will have even more information with which to profile us, and then to design ads that appeal to our most basic psychological needs in the best possible way. Even today, we are living in a dual reality: on one hand, we are concerned about the ability of companies to track us and attempt to manipulate us; on the other hand, we still willingly give up our privacy for the immediate benefits. Should it surprise us that people are ready to abandon significant elements of their life, such as privacy, for the sake of being able to order what they want or display and receive information? The truth is, people often make long-term sacrifices for short-term gains, such as putting their health at risk for the satisfaction of eating junk food, or staying in front of their computer rather than exercising.

Or, consider the potential negative aspects related to robots with emotional intelligence. Surely, they will be able to do great things and help in many places. However, who will set the borders between appropriate human–robot interaction, and what should be limited to interaction between human beings? Think about a robot capable of emotional intelligence living with an elderly man. Would we want the robot to be able to give him gentle feedback that he has forgotten to take his medication or that over the past few days he has been a bit distant from the people around him? Maybe. However, should we be concerned that, in our busy world focused on efficiency, the family of the old man visit him less frequently because "he has this great robot to take care of him." Consider the Spike Jonze film, *Her* (2013), in which the hero falls in love with the incredibly human software that he believes is in love with him, too? Now, think about a world in which you can design your romantic robotic partner. You can decide the color of the eyes, the type of body, in fact every physical and personality characteristic; this figment of your fantasy can become a reality. This leads to the question: Why bother with all the challenges that human relationships entail, when you can have the perfect partner?

This is actually not as bizarre as it sounds. A recent development that many of us will find frightening is the fact that, while the emotional intelligence of young people appears to be in decline, robots are actually demonstrating an increase in their emotional capabilities! In 2014, for example, at the University of Reading in the UK, an advanced computer program passed the Turing Test designed to differentiate between humans and robots. That is, it was perceived as being human. The answers provided by the program, which identified itself as a thirteen-year-old child from the Ukraine, managed to deceive the test administrators and it was not recognized as a robot. Judging by the amazing progress in this field, we may be looking at a future in which humans will increasingly fail the Turing Test while robots pass it.

Another concern is that the enhanced Internet experience (Internet of the five senses), while incredible, will boost Internet addiction. Adults and children may prefer to live online where life may be much more exciting than offline reality.

Another issue is the phenomenon of multitasking. Our ability to build and maintain intimacy with a significant other is already in decline as a result of doing too many things at once, and this situation can only get worse. Take, for example, Google glasses; wearing them enables the user to exist in the online and offline worlds simultaneously. It is not hard to imagine that this will be tremendously disruptive to your quality time with anyone, particularly your children.

The Internet of inanimate objects may have many positive features, but will it necessarily increase our sense of fun and enjoyment in life? Will it enhance our well-being? No, not necessarily. In fact, it is far more likely to make our lives more efficient and at the same time more demanding as we will be expected to do ever more.

In the light of the changes that are around the corner, as well as their pros and cons, we might consider the steps we can take in order to thrive in this new technological reality.

Technological developments are a double-edged sword. And which side we encounter depends on the values we adopt in relation to them, both as individuals and as a society.

LIGHTHOUSE VALUES

To return to the story of the encounter between the ship and the lighthouse, it is my belief that the tremendous speed with which technology has developed and continues to develop, together with the many commercial interests behind it, has created a storm and a fog, which are immensely difficult to navigate without the help of a lighthouse with a very strong beam. Sometimes, the fog can be deceptive: we don't realize that we are entering it until we are caught in its center. In the same way, we may not recognize that the privacy settings we apply on our computers are inadequate until our privacy has been compromised. To lead ourselves, and our society, to a safe shore, we need a lighthouse of real, unchanging values. (Recall that in the story it was the lighthouse that could not move, and the ship thus had to change course.) It is necessary to replace values such as efficiency and materialism with values that have greater worth and meaning. Below, I describe the values I advocate, and explain why they are necessary for our long-term psychological well-being.

People who seek greater well-being should focus on goals that involve growth and connection, rather than those that involve beauty, money, or popularity. In addition, these goals should involve contributing to others, and must be relevant and important to the individuals subscribing to them. Goals imposed by other people, or that are popular at the time, are difficult to achieve and have no personal meaning. This rule of thumb can also be applied when considering how to achieve individual well-being in relation to technology. Diener and Seligman (2002) compared happy with less happy people and found only one external factor distinguishing between them: the presence of satisfying social relationships. In other words, spending meaningful time with friends, family, and romantic partners is necessary for happiness. These two well-known figures in the field of positive psychology concluded that marriage and long-term cohabiting relationships have beneficial effects on well-being, as do family networks and intimate friendships. Belonging to a social group and being part of a community are also important factors. Community engagement has been shown to be a two-way street: it improves the lives of others while benefitting your own life. It is also circular, since involvement increases well-being and happy people tend to be more involved in their communities.

People have been shown to have three significant internal needs: *autonomy*, the feeling that your activities are self-chosen and self-endorsed; *competence*, feeling that you are effective in your activities;

and *relatedness*, feeling a sense of closeness with others (Deci & Ryan, 1985). The realization of these needs is crucial for behavioral self-regulation, personality development, and positive well-being. Of these, relatedness appears to be the most significant in terms of promoting a sense of well-being.

I adopted the values prescribed by SDT, with variations, as those of my lighthouse, using them as a means to examine each technological innovation to determine if it is being exploited in a positive or negative way – that is, whether it will enhance our well-being. My approach has received approval from Deci and Ryan.

Directing technology toward enhancing well-being requires effective, responsible guidance. My lighthouse values focus on autonomy, relatedness, social and global involvement, and competence.

Autonomy refers to the degree of freedom individuals experience and the feeling that they are in control of and can guide their lives – that is, self-governance. Philosopher Isaiah Berlin differentiated between positive and negative liberty ([1958] 1969). The former refers to the ability to direct and control our lives; the latter to the ability to remain free from the influence of others, be they individuals or institutions.

The western world has created unique challenges to the authentic expression of individuality. In agreement with psychologist Carl Rogers, I believe that our society creates role models that push us to adopt an ideal self that is not truly our own. Trying to achieve this false-self may well take us further and further from the fulfillment of our unique individuality. This situation is even more extreme online, particularly on social networks, because it is here that people increasingly derive their sense of self-esteem by receiving "likes" and "shares," and thus aim to express themselves in ways that will please and excite their online friends.

The first step towards achieving autonomy is self-awareness. You need to be aware of *your* true situation, and *your* real motivations. In order to do this you need to separate them from the beliefs and aspirations of other people – you must work out what belongs to you and what belongs to them. Then you will be able to set your own goals and achieve them. The process of becoming self-aware can be painful, because you have to study both your good points and achievements, and those parts of yourself that you like less. In order to be effective, it is important to emphasize your good points and achievements, which you want to build on and enhance, and frame the negative aspects as parts you're working on – mistakes you have grown from and those aspects of yourself that you may wish were different but have nonetheless accepted. It is very easy to sink into a negative place and cause your self-esteem to plummet, which is both destructive and leads to inertia and so is highly ineffective on every level.

Linked to this is the need to develop sound criteria and standards for analyzing and assessing your own thinking, and routinely using those criteria and standards to improve its quality (Elder & Paul, 1994). In essence, every individual needs to be able to think critically. Another definition of critical thinking relates to a conscious and deliberate process employed to evaluate or interpret evidence and experiences. This process is reflective and is used to direct beliefs and behaviors (Mertes, 1991). The ability to think critically will enable you to exercise your autonomy in the face of the onslaught of endless campaigns to persuade you to make purchases or buy into products and ideas that you would otherwise reject. With this in mind, below are some of the major questions that autonomous individuals ask themselves before committing to an idea or a product:

1. What is the purpose (i.e., goal) of this campaign?
2. What facts are being used to support its assertion? And have I examined these fully?
3. What are my needs and what alternative way exist to meet those needs?

When they are able to think critically, people will be better able to analyze the barrage of messages they receive from the media and choose whether to accept or reject them. Developing critical thinking skills is clearly not an easy task; however, they are necessary to maintaining our freedom and integrity.

CHATROOM: A SPECIAL CAMERA JUST FOR YOU

Last night Charlotte received an advertisement from an online site specializing in special, time-limited offers. This ad was just for her; it was even personally addressed. "Charlotte," it said, "you have won an opportunity to buy a uniquely special underwater camera." The camera had not yet hit the shops, the ad went on to explain, but as one of the site's "special members," she was being given the chance to be one of the first to own such a gorgeous piece of equipment, and at a special discounted price. However, there was a catch; as the ad explained, "This offer is available for 24 hours only, and the countdown has already begun." Accompanying the persuasive text was a photograph of a gorgeous young man and some examples of the fabulous images he had allegedly taken with the camera. The site also provided "genuine" feedback from three ecstatic customers.

Charlotte felt that this was too good an offer to miss out on. But, with credit card in hand and poised to input her details, she suddenly stopped and asked herself the following questions: What is the aim of this ad and how is it trying to influence me? How do I know that it is telling me the truth? Do those happy customers really exist? What evidence supports the claims in the ad? For example, is the price really a bargain? Maybe five other websites are also selling this camera, and their standard price may match this so-called "special offer." What about this personal, individualized pitch – is it genuine? Charlotte went on to consider the larger implications of the situation. Do I really need the recognition of a website to boost my self-esteem? What are my needs – is this ad answering them or imposing desires one me? Considering her responses to these questions, she duly put her credit card away, and felt a sense of relief sweep over her as she realized that her savings were still intact and she hadn't fallen into the trap set for her.

Internal motivation is also related to one's sense of autonomy. When we are aware of our own intrinsic motivators, we act according to our own beliefs and agenda, and not those of other people. Living a life directed by our internal motivations provides us with greater happiness and satisfaction, greater self-worth, and greater control over our lives. Certainly, negotiation and compromise are often necessary in relations with others. However, awareness of our internal motivators, and associated sense of autonomy, will inform our decisions regarding what is really important to us and what we are prepared to relinquish. People governed by external motivation are likely to shift position according to current fads; they are not true to themselves and thus lack a sense of coherence and consistency.

On the global scale, protecting our autonomy also involves an awareness of the power of online companies to access our data and manipulate our needs, desires, and sense of self-worth. A four-pronged strategic approach must be adopted when dealing with them:

1. Become aware of the dangers inherent in the way such companies use personal information.
2. Use online protest tools to put pressure on such companies to implement more transparent policies regarding the type of information they collect and how they use it. More power needs to be granted to the user to decide what these companies are allowed to do with personal information.
3. Encourage greater competition on the Internet and grant some form of quality standard recognition to those websites that aim to enhance the well-being of their users.
4. Regulate the power of Internet super companies.

Relatedness is another lighthouse value, which essentially refers to investing in family and close friends. In terms of better understanding ourselves and rooting ourselves in strong values, family and close friends are a major source of support and power. While the Internet facilitates keeping in touch with our loved ones, it can also blur the boundaries between real and online life and damage interpersonal relationships. Genuine intimacy is difficult to establish online, even though it may appear possible to feel an "immediate" connection with someone. The advent of the smartphone has made this situation even more salient, as people respond to messages in inappropriate circumstances, including when they are meant to be spending time with their partner or children. These relationships clearly suffer as a result. To modify an old adage: *On their deathbed, nobody has ever said, "I wish I'd spent more time on my smartphone."*

HOW DO WE OVERCOME COMMUNICATION TECHNOLOGY'S HOLD OVER OUR LIVES AND GOVERN ITS EFFECTS?

One approach to this conundrum is to create what I term *islands of love*, whereby one day a week we unplug ourselves from all forms of electronic communication – smartphones, tablets, and computers. This day is devoted to being ourselves, and to spending time with those close to us, without digital interference. It is focused on breathing, thinking, listening and being listened to, giving and receiving love, slowing down, and having fun.

"Mini islands of love" can take the form of family meals or intimate time with a close friend – when the smartphone is switched off and we are totally present. Behaving in this way may feel uncomfortable or embarrassing initially, for both parties. People are used to a different pattern of behavior and this sudden change may be a little unnerving. Evidence suggests that these actions are totally necessary, however. The quality of our connections with others will be positively transformed in a very short space of time and we'll probably ask ourselves why we hadn't taken action before. Improving interpersonal relations will also boost our sense of psychological well-being and, as a result, enhance our ability to deal with life's challenges.

Social and global involvement is another value I ascribe to the lighthouse. It is important to note that a mutual relationship exists between an individual and a group to which they belong. We want to receive support from the group and hope to give back in some sense too. Belonging to a group or a community allows us to give, and giving, perhaps surprisingly, is empowering and psychologically rewarding. According to US political scientist Robert Putnam (1982), communal involvement creates positive circular contact; that is, being engaged with one's community increases one's psychological well-being, and happy people tend to be more involved in their communities.

Here, I divide social involvement into two categories: the immediate community (offline) and the global village community (including online elements). Involvement in the immediate community means dedicating time and effort to others in your locality. It involves helping in traditional ways, such as visiting an elderly person who has no family, or helping new migrants learn your language. Global involvement means trying to have a positive impact on a community somewhere else in the world. We all have obligations to one another and to the global world, and chief among them is helping others, even though they are not in our geographical region, we are very unlikely to ever meet them, and they are certainly not likely to reciprocate.

CHATROOM: GOOD TECHNOLOGY

In the past, I strongly believed that technology is neither good nor bad, but relative – it's all a question of what you do with it, and people can utilize technology in ways that reflect their values. Recently, however, I became aware that some developers are intentionally creating technological services that will cause psychological harm to their users and possibly result in addiction.

I work at creating the opposite effect and harnessing technology for the benefit of humankind.

I run a university course in which students work in teams to create projects that will help in the global world. The scope, variety, and standard of the projects always astound me. Examples include websites to: help improve the self-image of people with brain damage; prompt people all over the world to keep their beaches clean; encourage young girls to study technology despite cultural stereotypes; and help people with autism to gain employment. Many of these students have brought together information from a whole variety of sources and centralized it within single websites in ways that have never existed before. My students have discovered that, when you change your vision from the immediate area to encompassing the world, and add a prosocial perspective and creativity, you can make a real impact – and that is extremely rewarding.

Hungarian psychologist Mihaly Csikszentmihalyi (1975) studied the peak experiences in life, when people know true happiness. He argues that such experiences result from being in a highly focused mental state in which we become totally absorbed in what we are doing. In order for this to happen, we have to lose ourselves in the experience and forget time and other pressures of daily life. Only then are we likely to experience a positive peak experience. Csikszentmihalyi termed such a peak experience, "flow."

Unfortunately, in the digital world we inhabit, it is increasingly hard to achieve flow. Even when out hiking or attending the opera, we are likely to encounter someone on their smartphone. We live in a world surrounded by electronic bleeps, buzzes, and flashing lights, which are not meant to disturb us, but do. And if we can't achieve flow, then we are never going to achieve the happiness that derives from peak experiences.

CHATROOM: PRESENT IN THE PRESENT

At an ancient Buddhist monastery in a hidden, hard-to-reach spot in India, monks hold a traditional ceremony every fifty years, which is intricate and exciting to watch. Hundreds of tourists made the difficult journey in order to witness the most recent ceremony. They assumed the best positions they could manage, and held up their cameras to record the event.

A young monk, astonished by their behavior, approached a tourist who was taking one photograph after another, and gently asked her what she was doing. Now it was the tourist's turn to be surprised, "Why, I am documenting this special event so that I will be able to share this extraordinary experience and memories with family and friends at home." The monk was even more astounded, and burst out, "But you, yourself, are not present now! How can you share an encounter that you never experienced?"

Our final lighthouse value is *competence*, which is important in terms of applying our values. It is the ability to translate our intentions into action. It is the move from dream to reality. Without competence we will remain only dreamers. Competence requires a sense of optimism and a well-thought-out strategy.

Optimism is a positive view of the world. Helen Keller, a writer and social activist, was also deaf and blind. Despite the difficulties this presented, she achieved a great deal in her life, and in my eyes is a role model for optimism. Keller said, "Optimism is the faith that leads to achievement; nothing can be done without hope and confidence." A sense of optimism will define your future world in a positive light. Some people are naturally more optimistic than others, but nonetheless it is a skill than can be learned. To develop a more optimistic outlook, we need to focus on goals that we set for ourselves and achieved, and label them successes. Thinking about these successes, no matter how small, transforms us into people who believe in our own ability to change. It is also important to be aware of our human and physical environments. We need to try to surround ourselves with people who are optimistic about themselves and have positive feelings towards us. Doing so will help us to fulfill ourselves as individuals and pursue our goals. Of course, life has a way of happening, and we will always encounter situations in which we cannot avoid people who have a negative impact on us; in these cases, we need an awareness of the precise effect these others create and this knowledge will automatically significantly lessen, or blunt, their effect. Designing our physical environment involves working to surround ourselves with stimuli that enhance our positive thinking and support us in our individual path. This can be done by placing inspiring books or pictures, for example, in your home and workplace – items that trigger a positive mindset.

When we attempt to identify and pursue our long-term goals, a *well-thought-out strategy* is necessary. We need to be both organized and ambitious. To make this happen, we must develop our self-efficacy; that is, our ability to complete tasks and achieve goals (Bandura, 1977). We must ask ourselves where we want to be one, three, or even five years from now. The aim should be both ambitious and realistic, which is a difficult balance to achieve. A target that is not sufficiently challenging or interesting is not likely to motivate us, while an over-ambitious goal may cause us to give up. The next phase is translating our targets into smaller, achievable sub-targets, which will lead us gradually to the long-term goal. These sub-targets need to be realistic, based on our abilities, while also incorporating an appropriate amount of "stretch" or ambition. Like a rubber band, we want to create a stretch that will be felt, but not one that will cause it to snap. In other words, we need to feel challenged, and also to experience success.

Keeping a written record of progress will greatly increase our chance of success. This testimony of our commitment will spur us on. Documenting our progress also means that we are more likely to engage in the vital act of rewarding ourselves for our achievements, both big and small. Self-recognition of our achievements is a pivotal factor in our success. Failures are also inevitable, and these should be understood as opportunities to learn and to change our behavior according to our conclusions to enhance our likelihood of success next time around. It is vital to learn from both successes and failures.

The path is long and we are likely to face challenges all the way along. This should not stop us. People grow psychologically by confronting life's challenges. As we move forward, step by step, our life becomes more meaningful for us.

A FINAL WORD

The digital world we inhabit is dynamic, challenging, and sometimes frightening. But we have many choices: we can choose to drift or be tossed around in our boat, at the mercy of the ocean, or we can invest in an effective navigation system. The lighthouse values, I believe, constitute the most effective and enduring method for navigating the digital storm. As we make significant progress, we become change agents in our own lives and a beacon for others.

REFERENCES

Amichai-Hamburger,Y., & Etgar, S. (2016). Intimacy and smartphone multitask-ing: A new oxymoron? *Psychological Reports*, 119 (3), 826-838.

Amabile, T. M., Constance, N. H., & Kramer, S. J. (2002). Creativity under the gun. *Harvard Business Review*, 80(8), 52–61.

Bandura,A. (1977). Self-efficacy: Toward a unifying theory of behavioral change. *Psychological Review*, 84(2), 191–215.

Berlin, I. ([1958] 1969). Two concepts of liberty. In *Four Essays on Liberty*. Oxford: Oxford University Press.

Covey, S. R. (1989). *The Seven Habits of Highly Effective People*. New York: Fireside, Simon & Schuster.

Csikszentmihalyi, M. (1975). *Beyond Boredom and Anxiety*. San Francisco, CA: Jossey-Bass.

Deci, E. L., & Ryan, R. M. (1985). *Intrinsic Motivation and Self-determination in Human Behavior*. New York: Plenum Press.

Diener, E., & Seligman, M. E. P. (2002).Very happy people. *Psychological Science*, 13, 81–84.

Elder, L., & Paul, R. (1994). Critical thinking: Why we must transform our teaching. *Journal of Developmental Education*, 18(1), 34–35.

Huxley,A. L. (1932). *Brave New World*. London: Chatto & Windus.

Kane, C. (2015).Why Americans just won't take time off. *Fortune*. http://fortune.com/2015/05/01/paid-time-off-vacation.

Kasser,T. (2002). *The High Price of Materialism*. Cambridge, MA: MIT Press.

Kasser,T., Ryan, R. M., Couchman, C. E., & Sheldon, K. M. (2004). Materialistic values:Their causes and consequences. In T. Kasser & A. D. Kanner (Eds.), *Psychology and Consumer Culture: The Struggle for a Good Life in a Materialistic World* (pp. 11–28).Washington, DC: American Psychological Association.

Mertes, L. (1991).Thinking and writing. *Middle School Journal*, 22, 24–25.

Orwell, G. (1949). *Nineteen Eighty-Four*. London: Secker & Warburg.

Postman, N. (1982). *The Disappearance of Childhood*. New York: Vintage.

Postman, N. (1985). *Amusing Ourselves to Death: Public Discourse in the Age of Show Business*. New York: Viking Penguin.

Postman, N. (1993). *Technopoly: The Surrender of Culture to Technology*. New York: Vintage Books.

Putnam, R. D. (2000). *Bowling Alone: The Collapse and Revival of American Community*. New York: Simon & Schuster.

Ryan, R. M., & Deci, E. L. (2000). Self-determination theory and the facilitation of intrinsic motivation, social development, and well-being. *American Psychologist*, 55, 68–78.

Seligman, M. E. P. (2002). *Authentic Happiness*. New York: Free Press.

Twenge, J. M. (2013). The evidence for generation me and against generation we. *Emerging Adulthood*, 1, 11–16.

GLOSSARY

Avatar A virtual computer character that is designed by the user to represent them in an online environment.

Blog An online journal written and edited by its owner, termed the blogger. By definition it is open to readers in accordance with the parameters defined by the blogger. It can be anonymous or identifiable.

Chat An online conversation carried out by text.

Email A text message transferred from one address to another in real time. The sender decides when to send the email and the recipient decides when to open it. As email use became more widespread, regular mail was termed snail mail.

Fantasy games An online environment that allows the user to become an active part of an adventure by using a virtual character (avatar) that they have created. The game is usually divided into several levels according to degree of complexity.

Forum An Internet website that enables a textual discussion group on a particular topic. Users can choose whether or not to participate in real time.

Google An Internet information search engine currently considered to be the most popular.

Online social networks An online group of people that interact with one another via the Internet. Facebook is the leading social network. Facebook users define their profiles as the image they want to present to the world. Personal information may include family status, personal photographs and hobbies. Individuals define their group through their acceptance (or not) of others as friends. Instagram is an online social network focused on photograph and video sharing. Twitter is an online social network for sending and reading short messages called "tweets." Tumblr is an online social network in the form of blogging.

Search engines Websites that facilitate finding information on the Internet using key words.

Second Life A virtual world that allows its users to enact a virtual character (avatar) of their creation and experience an environment that attempts to replicate the offline world. Variations on Second Life environments are designed mainly by users.

Skype An Internet service that enables real-time audio and visual interaction through a screen.

Tablet A flat-screen computer that does not have an external keyboard or mouse.

Talkback An Internet tool allowing users to react to news and express their opinions. It reflects the equality intrinsic to the Internet, while at the same time has led to public debate concerning whether online speech should be regulated.

YouTube An Internet website that allows people to upload and watch movies (ranging from amateur to professional) online. Popular movies have the potential to become viral, namely, to be seen by millions of people all around the world.

INDEX

Rosander, M. & Eriksson, O. 126
Rose, Elizabeth & Tim 12, 13
Ruesch, M. 161
rules: Facebook 21, 22; Internet 21; lack of enforcement 71; social networks 3

search engines 193*gl* see also Google
search options, "maximizers" and "satisfiers" 63
Second Life (game) 166, 167, 193*gl*
security and attachment theory 39–41
self-efficacy theory 138
self-esteem 4, 39–41, 95, 96
selfies 38
Seligmann, M. E. P. 176
sensation-seeking 41, 42
senses and virtual reality 177, 178, 180
sexism 85, 86–7
sexual harassment, normalization of 86
sexual violence 70, 71, 85, 86–7, 98
SIDE model (social identity model of deindividuation effects) 122, 123
Silberman, Steve 85
situational leadership theory 133
Skype 24, 25, 27, 91, 193*gl*
smartphones: accessibility and availability of Internet 7, 8, 174, 185, 187; and children and young people 91, 102, 107, 109; and cyberbullying 102; and groups 117; and intimacy 55, 186; and online love 52
Snowden, Edward 84
social anxiety 31
social identity model of deindividuation effects see SIDE model
social learning theory (Bandura) 68–70, 76, 98

social loafing 128–30
social networks online 193*gl*; and attachment 40; idealized profiles 4, 5; and narcissism 38; and personality type 33, 34; rules 3; sensation-seeking behavior 41; and social identity 34
social relationships, importance of 181
social restraints, lack of online 75, 76
social status, instability of 16
social taboos 49
social tradeoffs 48
speed 10, 11, 12
Spitzberg, Brian & Cupach, William 64
Stafford, Cheryl 154
status symbols, traditional 10
stereotyping 86, 87, 151, 155–7, 163, 164–7
suicide: and cyberbullying 70, 103; online assessment of risk 25; risk of missing intent 25, 26
superego 21
surveillance 84, 85
Swift, Taylor 64

tablets 193*gl*
Tactical Ops: Assault on Terror (game) 99
Tajfel, H., Billig, M. G., Bundy, R. P. & Flament, C. 121, 122
Talkback 9, 14, 193*gl*
terrorist organizations 77–80, 81; and aim to arouse fear 80; funding and Internet 80, 81; 9/11 80; sale of young girls 81
totalitarian regimes 132
transformational leadership 138
trust and intimacy 56, 57
Tumblr 64, 193*gl*
Tuvako, Stanley 151